MESSAGE

TO

THE BLACK MAN

II

God Has A Word For You

Malak Yesha'Yahu ben Yahudah

ISBN: 978-1-7376879-0-0

i

DEDICATION

This book is dedicated to The Most High God of Abraham, Isaac and Jacob. Yahuah T'Sebaoth, the Elohim of the slaves, the Great and Terrible Elohim who keeps Covenant and shows mercy to those of His people that love Him and keep His Commandments. The Creator of the Universe who has said that Israel is His first-born son.

Your judgements are altogether righteous. And Your chastening has been well deserved. Now Abba Yah we return to You.

To His Son Yahshua or Yahusha or Yahowashi ha'Maschiach the only begotten Son of Yahuah. Our soon and coming King that laid down His life as a ransom for the whole House of Israel.

To the Ruach ha'Kodesh our Comforter and Guide sent to lead us and guide us back to Aluah the only True and Living Elohim.

I bow before you and none else. I repent on behalf of myself, my family and forefathers in that we did not harken unto Your voice. And for this cause we are trapped in captivity until we return to You the Elohim of our Salvation. Who through the hardships our people have endured has awakened us, the Negro to our true identity,

> *"Is Israel a servant? Is he a homeborn slave? Why is he spoiled?*

Jeremiah 2:14

I thank You for the great awakening of Your people to our true identity. And allowing us, Your Chosen People the so called "Negro" aka Israelites aka Hebrews one last opportunity to chose You over fake white jesus and the imposters pretending to be us. Thank you Abba Yah. I love You. We love You and give You all the Glory, Honor and Praise.

Amen

Family Dedication

To my parents Charles and Janet. To Pops who only spoke when something needed to be said, like "if you ever go to jail don't call here" or "you better be in the yard before the street lights come on." "What time do the lights come on Dad." "I don't know but you better be in the yard before they come on." Who never once said I love you but showed it by going to work every day and never complained one time about the cards he was dealt.

And to Mom who never shut up and was big Mama to all those that needed a good word. She always said, "you gonna miss me when I'm gone. Who had an "ism" for every situation, like, "Y'all don't believe fat meat's greasy" or "I'm gon beat you 'til your nose bleeds" or "a hard head makes for a soft behind." They were unbeknownst to me and my siblings the most amazing upbringing one could ever as for. I miss you like crazy and wish you knew who you were before leaving this earth. I love you both. RIP

To my wife, children, brothers, sister and family some of whom that are not yet in the Truth and have yet to accept the true Besorah of that Negro name Jesus or Yahshua. May you all awaken as I have to the truth of who we are as the Chosen of Yahuah our Abba Yah.

To the one third of my people that will accept the Truth and return to the Laws, Statutes and Commands of the The Most High (TMH).

And to the Gentiles and Strangers that will cleave to the House of Israel as servants in the life to come.

CONTENTS

PREFACE ix

WHY 1

    The Why Question 1

    The Bottoms Up Club, the Fight for Equal Rights 5

    A Little Bit of This, a Little Bit of That 8

    Let's Begin at the Beginning 12

    Happy to be Nappy 13

    Did Yahshua Teach Israel to Keep the Law? 18

    Yahshua We Know, But Who Are You? 19

WHO DOES HE LOOK LIKE? WHO DO WE LOOK
LIKE? 32

    Heavenly Father, is that You? 32

    The Talk Game 33

    Abba Yah's and His Talk Game 36

    Roll Tape 42

    Who 'da People? 45

    Breadcrumbs Please 48

The Deuteronomy 28:68 Controversy 50

Calling Fire Down on Our Heads 54

WHERE Y'ALL FROM? **58**

Negro, Nigger, and NEGROLAND 62

Greatest Identity Theft of All Time 65

King Joseph's Letter to Rabbi Shaprut 66

Speaking in Tongues 69

Can the Imposters Do That? 72

The Bottom Line 76

Why Does It Matter? 80

The Constantine Hijack 83

Who You 'wit? The Case Against Fake White Jesus 88

Mixing the Holy with the Profane 91

The Christian Church is the Church of Satan? 98

Know Them by Their Fruit 101

Deal with the Devil 102

They Steal 104

You Lookin' for Me? 107

They kill 111

They destroy 114

Neanderthal French for Nephilim or Fallen Angels? 116

His People, his people... 123

You Twitchin' Baby, You Twitchin'................................ 126

We Must Return to Our Heritage.......................... 127

THE ANSWER 135

Grand Rising.. 135

So What We 'Gon Do? 143

The Covenant,.. 155

The Reaffirmation,.. 155

The Rulership,... 156

Ain't Nothin' Like the Real Thing, Baby 158

The Destroyer of the Gentiles is on His Way 160

The Final Solution 170

PREFACE

"Who are you?

What was your name?

And why don't you know now what your name was then?"

Malcolm X

Dear Black man (aka Negro),

What if I told you everything you have been taught is a lie? What if I told you that everything in this world is BIBLICAL? What if I told you that the Bible was all about you and everyone else is secondary? What if I told you that there really are people in very high places who have conspired to keep you from the knowledge of who you are?

In the next few minutes, I will show you that the so-called NEGROES are the single most important people on the planet. That, in fact, when they say we should be watching Israel as God's time clock, they should be watching the Black man, aka Negro, aka Israelite, aka Hebrew, and not the people living in your land pretending to be you. I will show you that you are indeed the true chosen people of the Creator of the heavens and the earth. And this has all been about the biggest case of identity theft in human history.

We will explore how it is that the Black man has no history and no land. We will explore how that happened and why it happened. Unlike most things in our community, this book will not only talk about why the so-called Black man is where he is, but most importantly, it will offer the only solution available to us.

However, before we begin our journey, let us start by saying that this book and this teaching is not designed for everyone. It is ONLY designed for those that have been CHOSEN by The Most High God, aka Yahuah, the Elohim of Abraham, Isaac, and Jacob, and no one else. Yahuah T'Sebaoth is His name. Others say His name is so sacred it cannot be said. Nothing is further from the truth. He says His name over and over again in the

Scripture. Some others say His name is too sacred to say because His name was never given to them in the first place. They cannot call upon a God to whom they are sworn enemies.

> *"For Esau is the end of the world, and Jacob is the beginning of it that followeth."*
>
> 2 Esdras 6:9

So, His name is kept out of their mouths because they are not His people. His name is reserved for His people and those that cleave to His people. In the Black community, when someone is talking bad about us, what do we say? We say, 'You better keep my name out of your mouth.' God, the Lord of Hosts, aka TMH Yah, aka Yahuah T'Sebaoth, has done exactly that. He has kept His name out of their mouth. And has reserved His name for His people and His people alone. SAY HIS NAME Black man. Say His name Israel...Yahuah T'Sebaoth.

WHY

The Why Question

The question before us as Black people is WHY? Our babies have the ability to cut through the nonsense and ask the seminal question... WHY?

And if you think back to when you were a child and remember the first time you saw your people being disrespected, the question you asked was WHY? I remember my father being called boy by an old shriveled up white woman and thinking, WHY is this woman calling my dad, a grown man, boy? At that time, I was still young enough not to understand the black-white dynamic, but I understood enough to know that it was not cool to hear some really old white woman calling my dad boy. I am sure in his mind, with all the daily pitfalls that come with being a Black man in a racist society, that was the least of his worries. She looked old enough to be his grandmother.

And after all, coming from Georgia, he had the real memory of the stories of my great-great-grandfather being beaten, shot, hung, and set on fire in front of his wife and children for the crime of helping a brother on the run from the Klan. A fact that sadly he had no knowledge of until the Klan showed up with their bloodhounds tracking the other brother. And it didn't help that his wife looked white even though she was still considered Negro. It means she herself was the product of the rape of her mother or grandmother.

The absolute terror and torture our people lived through at the hands of these people that can and do murder, steal, and kill throughout the week and then go to church on Sunday to thank God for all their blessings is incomprehensible. Who can do this and think there is no judgment coming for them and/or their offspring?

> *"4 Thus saith the LORD my God; Feed the flock of the slaughter;*
>
> *5 Whose possessors slay them, and hold themselves not guilty: and they that sell them say, Blessed be the LORD; for I am rich: and their own shepherds pity them not."*
>
> Zechariah 11:4-5

Their conscience has been seared in such a way that they cannot see their own wickedness and depravity. They believe their every evil work is a command and a blessing from the God of Abraham, Isaac, and Jacob. Our Elohim has said,

> *"21 These things hast thou done, and I kept silence; thou thoughtest that I was altogether such an one as thyself: but I will reprove thee, and set them in order before thine eyes."*
>
> Psalms 50:21

It's not like they don't understand the concept of recompense. Thomas Jefferson, Rapist-in-Chief, was even quoted as saying, "Can the liberties of a nation be secure when we have removed a conviction that these liberties are the gift of God? Indeed, I tremble for my country when I reflect that God is just and that His justice cannot sleep forever."

So, if you know there is a judgment for wrongdoing, WHY continue it on this scale? Unless, of course, it's in your DNA, and you cannot help it. Even when they attempt to do right, they end up wrong because hidden within their genetic code is the propensity for evil, as we shall see.

Have you asked yourself as a so-called Black person why we are so screwed up as a people?

We repeatedly hear ad nauseum that we as Black people are at the bottom of society no matter where we are located in the world. And the sad truth is, this is correct. Whatever negative statistic you look at, so-called Blacks seem to lead the way here in the US, and just about everywhere we are found.

WHY?

The Bottoms Up Club, the Fight for Equal Rights

Historically, the poverty rate in the community has been about 25-30%. Since being emancipated from slavery, our poverty rate has been 2-3 times that of whites. Time and again, since emancipation, Black leaders have tried to get the government to address many of the inequities in this society to little or no avail.

Frederick Douglass, the great orator, and abolitionist did his best to bring the issues of inequity to the forefront in the late 1800s. He made small gains, but in the end, Jim Crow supplanted the reconstruction.

After Douglass' death came Marcus Mosiah Garvey. Through the Universal Negro Improvement Association

(UNIA), Garvey attempted to lift the social, political, and economic outlook for Black people in the US and around the world. He gained great notoriety and progress for our people until the government stepped in and began a sabotage and harassment campaign that ended with him being convicted of a non-crime, imprisoned, and eventually deported back to Jamaica.

But the die was cast by Garvey, and the search for freedom, equality, and justice was on. We then have the truly great Malcolm X or, as Ossie Davis said, "Our Manhood." His parents were part of the Garvey movement. So, Malcolm's early life was informed by Garvey.

Even the Honorable Elijah Muhammad was reportedly involved in Garvey's UNIA, although Minister Louis Farrakhan disputes this. Whatever the case may be, much of the Garvey platform is indeed shared by Elijah Muhammad's Nation of Islam, who espoused the same "Do for Self" ideology.

But back to Malcolm. He preached that Black people should demand their rights "by any means necessary." And once again, the government and its agents stepped in to cause strife and ultimately brought about Brother Malcolm's assassination either directly or indirectly.

During Malcolm's time, there was an even more prominent figure in the struggle for Civil Rights – Dr. Martin Luther King, Jr. Dr. Martin Luther King, Jr. was the greatest American orator, Black or White of his day. He mobilized Blacks as never before to demand that the so-called Negroes be integrated into mainstream White society.

Under Dr. King, the momentum and march towards equality was unstoppable culminating in the Civil Rights Movement of the 1950s and 1960s, which reached a crescendo with the March on Washington led by Dr. King.

However, even with all the efforts made by Black leadership, we are still on the bottom looking up. Before his assassination, Dr. King was quoted as saying, "I fear I may have integrated my people into a burning house."

Martin Luther King tried. Malcolm X tried. Marcus Garvey tried. Patrice Lumumba tried. Kwame Nkrumah tried. Nelson and Winnie tried. Jomo Kenyatta tried. As did countless others try to reason with our oppressors. But in the end, they could not free us from the European slave masters and colonialists' grip. And, we are still today at the bottom of society anywhere we may be found.

But the question still remains...

WHY?

Why do Americans and Europeans, in general, have little to no problem assimilating every culture, every race, and every religion except when it came to the so-called Black man? Why? What have we done to be so poorly treated by not just Europeans but every group of people from the Europeans to the Arabs who still operate an open-air slave market today that enslaves ONLY West Africans? As well as Asians who set up shop in Black neighborhoods and proceed to mistreat and in many cases physically attack the very Black people that keep them in business. To Arabs and East Indians that profit from the mini-mart and gas stations. To Ashkenazi Jews that steal every dollar possible from our people through the entertainment industry making billions off our community's talents while the Black people responsible for the talents end up broken and destroyed. What's going on here? Why is that?

A Little Bit of This, a Little Bit of That

As so-called Negroes, we have tried a little bit of everything in an effort to improve our situation and station in life. The system we live in has kept our heads spinning as we are told that we are where we are because we don't do this or that. We do too much of this and not enough of that.

They started off telling us that we were nothing but a bunch of uncivilized savages running around butt naked in the jungles of Africa. And it took the White man to rescue us from our savage state of mind. They told us slavery was actually an improvement over our animalistic behavior. The audacity of people to try to teach other people these kinds of lies about themselves. However, just as Hitler said, 'If you tell a lie long enough and strong enough, the people will believe.'

And so, we believed. But Malcolm asked the question in a speech given in Los Angeles about police brutality, "What was your name? What were you before the White man named you Negro? And what did you have? What was your language?"

We live among people that have erased our history before slavery and replaced it with a Eurocentric narrative that never allows us to go any further back than slavery. Every year in America, we rehash the same two or three people that taught us to bow down and accept our current situation as God's will for us as lesser people. But Malcolm's question deserves answers.

However, in America and really in the rest of the Negro world, we were given religion instead of answers. We were lulled to sleep with the soothing words of the sweet by and by. A land called Beulah Land. A land of milk and honey, way over there on the other side. If we were just good enough, a white man named Jesus would carry us over to the other side. As good, obedient, faithful, and dutiful slaves, we accepted Western European Style Christianity as the way out.

During slavery, Massa would even show up to hear the Sunday sermon given by one of his trusted slaves. We, of course, did not understand that Massa was there to make sure he didn't go off script like Nat Turner did. The funny thing is, when we accepted the European version of Christianity, we were still treated as second-class citizens in the Kingdom of Heaven too. Only this time, we were told that we were of the seed of Ham. And that the curse of Ham was upon us, and we were consigned to slavery as a punishment for his sin against Noah. Damn! We can't win for losing... that is if we continue to listen to the wrong voice.

Well, if Constantine or Western European Style Christianity offers no real solution, what about Islam? While Constantine Christianity accounts for most blacks' religious affiliation, Islam is the second most popular religion. Many point out to us that we were Muslims and were forced to convert to Constantine Christianity.

The only problem with that analysis is that the Bible says the first believers were spread to Ethiopia more than six hundred years before Islam was ever thought of as a religion. Islam, like all these religions, was not a religion of choice but a religion of force. Before our people ever showed up in the Americas, they lived through Western European Style Christianity and Islam's forced conversions.

And for those that don't know, there is a difference between the Christianity of the Scripture and the Western European Style Christianity taught now. Let's look at that difference.

Let's Begin at the Beginning

We see that Yahshua ha'Maschiach of Scripture has always been with us. He was there at the very beginning with The Most High Abba Yah and is the "One" that Abba Yah was referring to when He said let "US" make man in "OUR" image. When you read the Paleo Hebrew (remember Paleo reads from right to left), you find that the Son was there in the beginning:

'Elohyim bara' B-re'shyit"

(God) (created)(In the beginning)

'eth

(first and last)

"ha'eretz wa-'eth hashamyim

(earth) (and first and last) (heavens)

In the two places where "'eth" appears, the two letters of this word are the first and the last letters in the Hebrew aleph-beyt, the aleph and the tav. When we look at what Yahshua ha'Maschiach said about Himself, we find that hidden in the very first verse of the Scripture is Yahshua, aka Jesus,

> "13 *I am Alpha and Omega, the beginning and the end, the first and the last.*"

Revelation 22:13

Modern Hebrew acknowledges the word in most cases because it was there, but because the Bible is not their book, they have no understanding of the significance of the word, and they downplay its importance in biblical understanding, which reveals that Yahshua ha'Maschiach was with the Father all along. And this is the reason why the Scripture goes on to say,

> "26 *And God said, Let US make man in OUR image, after OUR likeness:*"

Genesis 1:26

This word "'eth" made up of the first and last letters of the Paleo Hebrew aleph-beyt speaks of Yahshua ha'Maschiach the Alpha and the Omega, beginning and the end at the beginning from the very first sentence. How is it hidden from their knowledge and understanding, unless this Word was never their Word, to begin with, but was stolen from other people to whom it belongs?

Happy to be Nappy

The biblical description of ha'Maschiach is on these verses:

"12 And I turned to see the voice that spake with me. And being turned, I saw seven golden candlesticks;

13 And in the midst of the seven candlesticks one like unto the Son of man, clothed with a garment down to the foot, and girt about the paps with a golden girdle.

14 His head and His hairs were white like wool, as white as snow; and His eyes were as a flame of fire;

15 And his feet like unto fine brass, as if they burned in a furnace; and his voice as the sound of many waters.

16 And he had in his right hand seven stars: and out of his mouth went a sharp two-edged sword: and his countenance was as the sun shineth in his strength.

17 And when I saw him, I fell at his feet as dead. And he laid his right hand upon me, saying unto me, Fear not; I am the first and the last:

18 I am he that liveth, and was dead; and, behold, I am alive forevermore, Amen; and have the keys of hell and of death."

Revelation 1:12-18

Two things we find is this same WOOLLY HAIR descriptor in the description of The Ancient of Days, aka Yahuah, Abba Yah, Heavenly Father, God Himself, as we find in Daniel 7:9. The same woolly hair used to describe Yahuah's hair is used to describe the Son of man's hair. So when you see woolly hair in the earth realm, you are seeing the sign of Yah's creation. All this time, we have been taught to hate our woolly hair only to find out at the end that our woolly hair is not a curse but a crown. Abba Yah crowned His creation with the same woolly hair that

14

He has on His head. Instead of being ashamed of our woolly hair, we need to celebrate it the way we did in the 1960s and 1970s.

When I was a very little boy, James Brown put out a record called, "Say it Loud, I'm Black and I'm Proud." I bought that record from the brother selling ice cream from the ice cream truck in our neighborhood. I took the record to school to show to my black friends at school. It was an all-white school with a very small population of black kids. All my little friends gathered around excitedly to look at my new record. The white teacher must have been watching us from across the playground because she came over to me and took the record away from me.

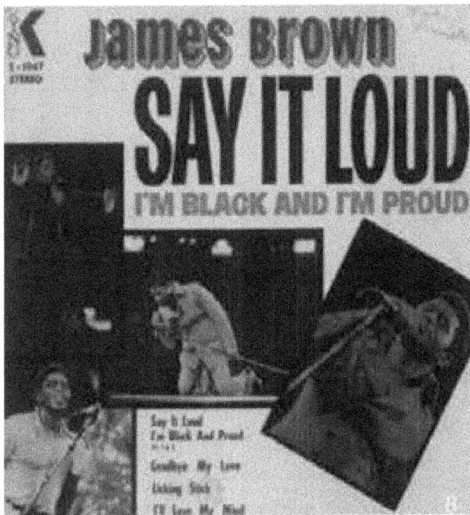

That record along with that slogan and others like it such as "Black is Beautiful," gave us the pride in ourselves that was anathema to the larger white society. Our Afros, tight shirts, dashiki's, bell-bottom pants, and revolutionary Black Panther talk scared the white community to death, especially those Afros. It was the one thing that was decidedly NEGRO and separated us from everyone else. When white folks started copying our hairstyle, I'm sure it sent shockwaves through the halls of white power in Washington. Those Afros, though; I can feel the beat now. I can hear James now,

"Say it Loud. I'm Black and I'm proud."

As we return to our heritage and our Elohim, aka our God, let us also return to the crown TMH Abba Yah gave us. That crown is that woolly hair that came directly from our Elohim, Yahuah, The Ancient of Days. Instead of being ashamed of our nappy hair, let us be,

"HAPPY TO BE NAPPY"

Yahshua ha'Maschiach is the One that is described as having hair like wool and skin the color of burnt brass.

Who did He come for?

Yahshua ha'Maschiach is the One that said,

> "*21 Then Jesus went thence, and departed into the coasts of Tyre and Sidon.*
>
> *22 And, behold, a woman of Canaan came out of the same coasts, and cried unto him, saying, Have mercy on me, O Lord, thou Son of David; my daughter is grievously vexed with a devil.*
>
> *23 But he answered her not a word. And his disciples came and besought him, saying, Send her away; for she crieth after us.*
>
> *24 But he answered and said, I am not sent but unto the lost sheep of the House of Israel.*"
>
> *Matthew 15:24*

In the coming pages, we will find out who exactly the lost sheep is based on Scripture. The Scripture points out exactly who these people are.

He is the One that kept the Sabbath and the Law while here on earth.

Did Yahshua Teach Israel to Keep the Law?

Is not this Yahshua ha'Maschiach the same One that told the rich young man that asked Him what he must do to enter into the kingdom that said,

> "*17 And He said unto him, Why callest thou Me good? there is none good but One, that is, God: but if thou wilt enter into life, keep the commandments.*"
>
> *Matthew 19:17*

Then at the end, He says in multiple places,

> "*17 And the dragon was wroth with the woman, and went to make war with the remnant of her seed, which keep the commandments of God, and have the testimony of Jesus Christ.*"
>
> *Revelation 12:17*

And,

> "*12 Here is the patience of the saints: here are they that keep the commandments of God, and the faith of Jesus.*"

Revelation 14:12

And,

> *"14 Blessed are they that do His commandments, that they may have right to the tree of life, and may enter in through the gates into the city."*

Revelation 22:14

Here we find that the true Messiah, aka ha'Maschiach kept the Commandments and told others that if they would enter into life, they must keep the Commandments. Something the Constantine or Western European Style Christians teach against. So, who are you going to believe? The Messiah or Constantine Christians?

Yahshua We Know, But Who Are You?

Paul warned of another Yahshua or Jesus for those that changed His name,

> *"2 For I am jealous over you with godly jealousy: for I have espoused you to one husband, that I may present you as a chaste virgin to Christ.*
>
> *3 But I fear, lest by any means, as the serpent beguiled Eve through his subtilty, so your minds should be corrupted from the simplicity that is in Christ.*
>
> *4 For if he that cometh preacheth another Jesus, whom we have not preached, or if ye receive another spirit, which ye have not received, or another gospel, which ye have not accepted, ye might well bear with him."*

19

2 Corinthians 11:2-4

This fake white Jesus has been carefully packaged and sold to us as the Savior of the world. This is that other Yahshua or Jesus that neither Paul nor the apostles ever preached. This fake white Jesus says that he came for everyone.

Fake white Jesus is full of fun and blessings with no judgment. No matter how heinous the crime or the sin.

He is the one that a Black Pastor said because of fake white Jesus, it is a sin to keep the Law. And that there is no need to keep the Sabbath.

The image of fake white Jesus has been used to lead our people away from following the Laws, Statutes, and Commands of Yah to following the dictates of satan and his style of worship, which is to forgo the keeping of the Sabbath. And to set aside Abba Yah's Feast Days in favor of Ishtar's worship (pronounced Easter) and the birth of her child Tammuz nine months later known as Christmas. So while we have been given the story that these things are part of biblical Christianity, they are done in direct contradiction to the Word of Abba Yah.

Upon closer inspection of the Western European version of Christianity, we find that almost all of their worship practices are pagan Baal worship practices. Taking pagan worship practices and calling them worship practices of The Most High is an abomination. When the children of Israel left Egypt and were awaiting Moses' return, they made themselves a golden calf to worship, thinking they were worshipping God,

"¹ And when the people saw that Moses delayed to come down out of the mount, the people gathered themselves together unto Aaron, and said unto him, Up, make us gods, which shall go before us; for as for this Moses, the man that brought us up out of the land of Egypt, we wot not what is become of him.

² And Aaron said unto them, Break off the golden earrings, which are in the ears of your wives, of your sons, and of your daughters, and bring them unto me.

³ And all the people brake off the golden earrings which were in their ears, and brought them unto Aaron.

⁴ And he received the mat their hand, and fashioned it with a graving tool, after he had made it a molten calf: and they said, These be thy gods, O Israel, which brought thee up out of the land of Egypt.

⁵ And when Aaron saw it, he built an altar before it; and Aaron made proclamation, and said, Tomorrow is a feast to the LORD."

Exodus 32:1-5

Just because you worship does not mean you are worshipping the God of Abraham, Isaac, and Jacob.

Fake white Jesus is another Yahshua or Jesus that Paul warned of in Scripture. This fake white Jesus is the image of the beast spoken of,

"¹¹ And I beheld another beast coming up out of the earth; and he had two horns like a lamb, and he spake as a dragon.

21

12 And he exerciseth all the power of the first beast before him, and causeth the earth and them which dwell therein to worship the first beast, whose deadly wound was healed.

13 And he doeth great wonders, so that he maketh fire come down from heaven on the earth in the sight of men,

14 And deceiveth them that dwell on the earth by the means of those miracles which he had power to do in the sight of the beast; saying to them that dwell on the earth, that they should make an image to the beast, which had the wound by a sword, and did live.

15 And he had power to give life unto the image of the beast, that the image of the beast should both speak, and cause that as many as would not worship the image of the beast should be killed."

Revelation 13:11-15

This fake white Jesus has been given to us complete with a fake pagan worship system that tells us that there is no longer any need to keep the Sabbath or the Law. Yet in those books that were kept out of the Scripture approved by the seed of Satan, we find that the Sabbath has been kept in heaven from before the foundation of the world. And was only passed on to the children of Israel as a sign of Abba Yah's love and Covenant with us,

"16 And He finished all His work on the sixth day--all that is in the heavens and on the earth, and in the seas and in the abysses, and in the light and in the darkness, and in everything.

17 And He gave us a great sign, the Sabbath day, that we should work six days, but keep Sabbath on the seventh day from all work.

18 And all the angels of the presence, and all the angels of sanctification, these two great classes--He hath hidden us to keep the Sabbath with Him in heaven and on earth.

22

[19] And He said unto us: "Behold, I will separate unto Myself a people from among all the peoples, and these will keep the Sabbath day, and I will sanctify them unto Myself as My people, and will bless them; as I have sanctified the Sabbath day and do sanctify (it) unto Myself, even so shall I bless them, and they will be My people and I shall be their God.

[20] And I have chosen the seed of Jacob from amongst all that I have seen, and have written him down as My firstborn son, and have sanctified him unto Myself for ever and ever; and I will teach them the Sabbath day, that they may keep Sabbath thereon from all work."

[21] And thus He created therein a sign in accordance with which they should keep Sabbath with us on the seventh day, to eat and to drink, and to bless Him who hath created all things as He hath blessed and sanctified unto Himself a peculiar people above all peoples, and that they should keep Sabbath together with us."

Jubilees 2:16-21

So, who is fake white Jesus to say to Israel that there is no need to keep the Sabbath when it has been observed in heaven before the earth was established? Because there is NO COVENANT with the Gentiles, they tell us not to keep the Sabbath. But it was not so from the beginning.

It is fake white Jesus that did away with the Sabbath and Abba Yah's Holy Days in favor of Sunday worship and Ishtar (pronounced Easter) and Christmas holy days, complete with egg-laying bunny rabbits and Christmas trees deck out in gold and silver which the Scripture clearly warns us against in Jeremiah 10,

"² Thus saith the LORD, Learn not the way of the heathen, and be not dismayed at the signs of heaven; for the heathen are dismayed at them.

³ For the customs of the people are vain: for one cutteth a tree out of the forest, the work of the hands of the workman, with the axe.

⁴ They deck it with silver and with gold; they fasten it with nails and with hammers, that it move not.

⁵ They are upright as the palm tree, but speak not: they must needs be borne, because they cannot go. Be not afraid of them; for they cannot do evil, neither also is it in them to do good."

Jeremiah 10:1-5

So, where did all this paganism and false worship come from? If Paul warned us of another Jesus, how did we end up with another Jesus?

To get the answer, we must go back to the introduction of Europeans into Christianity. When Yahshua resurrected and was

24

taken up into heaven, the early Christians continued with the same Laws, Statutes, and Commands that they had before. Only now they incorporated the Messiah or ha'Maschiach into their worship. However, it wasn't long before the heathen or the Gentiles were attempting to steal the identity of the children of Israel and make our identity their identity,

> *"48 And laid open the book of the law, wherein the heathen had sought to paint the likeness of their images."*

> *1 Maccabees 3:48*

Paul had been entrusted with delivering the Gospel to the Gentiles. Paul dutifully delivered the Word of Yah to the Gentiles. Because there is no Covenant with the Gentiles, over time, they reverted to their culture. Study the Roman Emperor Constantine, who embraced Christianity with some spiritual gentrification, if you will. After hundreds of years of persecuting the Church that was essentially a Black religion as the Hebrews were a Black people, Constantine had suddenly gotten religious because of a vision that he had before going into a major battle against Emperor Maxentius where he was vastly overmatched but managed to win the battle, Constantine reversed course on the Roman policy of persecution of the early Christian Church which again was an essentially a Black religion. Europeans being Europeans meant that they could not countenance the worship of a Black God, so as a part of the Council of Nicaea in

325 AD, they replaced the Black Christ with an image of a god Ptolemy created some five or six hundred years earlier called Serapis Christus. Constantine and the Bishops at Nicaea used this Greco-Egyptian god as the new Christian god named Iesous Christos or Jesus Christ. This was the first attempt at recasting the Black Christ into a European. It was the first and would not be the last.

There was also controversy over when to celebrate the resurrection of Jesus Christ or Yahshua ha'Maschiach, which Constantine addressed. After much debate, it was decided that rather, keep the Passover date as the celebration of The Resurrection, the Europeans in charge went with Ishtar (pronounced Easter) as the date because they felt the Hebrews were guilty of the sin of crucifying Yahshua ha'Maschiach or Jesus as they called him. Overlooking the fact that they were the ones that actually pulled the trigger, so to speak. Constantine even had the unmitigated gall to say in a written letter to the Bishops that could not attend,

> *"It was, in the first place, declared improper to follow the custom of the Jews in the celebration of this holy festival, because, their hands having been stained with crime, the minds of these wretched men are necessarily blinded. Let us, then, have nothing in common with the Jews, who are our adversaries. Let us studiously avoiding all contact with that evil way. For how can they entertain right views on any point who, after having compassed the death of the Lord, being out of their minds, are guided not by sound reason, but by an unrestrained*

passion, wherever their innate madness carries them. lest your pure minds should appear to share in the customs of a people so utterly depraved. Therefore, this irregularity must be corrected, in order that we may no more have anything in common with those parricides and the murderers of our Lord. No single point in common with the perjury of the Jews."

- Constantine's letter to the Bishops who did not attend the Council of Nicaea conference

Is this dude serious? Don't get me wrong, our forefathers were the ones that authorized the crucifixion of Christ, but these folks sneered at our forefathers with actual blood on their hands. A practice they continue to this day. But who gave Constantine the authority?

Now that the true Israelites, who were black, and the early Christian converts were pushed to the side, the Europeans could go about the real work of turning the Negro Christ into a blonde-haired blue-eyed superhero. One of the things that our European enemies are to be commended for is their ability to plan far ahead. They plan at least one to two generations ahead while most of our people live day to day. We think a five-year plan shows amazing foresight. But when you rely on The Most High, there is no real need for long-term planning as long as you are walking in line with His Laws, Statutes, and Commands. If you're not, then Yah help you because no amount of planning will help you or save you.

Cesare Borgias = The False Image Of Jesus Christ

Fast forward to Pope Alexander VI, who had an illegitimate son by the name of Cesare Borgia. This Pope and his band of misfit offspring were so wicked that they even made a TV series named after them to capture and celebrate their debauchery called "Borgia." Never mind the fact that Popes were sworn to a life of celibacy, this Mac Daddy Pope had at least seven or eight kids and one by his own daughter. If there is one thing Euros love to do, it's celebrating evil and wickedness. And the Borgia's were among the most wicked.

Besides all the murder and intrigue associated with this family, perhaps the most heinous act was to have Leonardo DaVinci paint the Pope's favorite son in Christ's image. Up until the Renaissance period, nearly all the images of Biblical characters were painted as Black people. Even the images of God Himself were painted as Black and/or Negroid.

Why?

Because they lifted the images of Yahuah T'Sebaoth straight from the pages of Scripture. Daniel 7:9 says that the Ancient of Days who is none other than Yahuah or God the Father has WOOLLY HAIR. And Revelation 4:2-3 says the One who sits on the Throne has dark reddish skin tone. These descriptions come straight out of the Scripture. They are not made up.

But once again, Europeans being the seed of Satan that they are, sought to change the image of Abba Yah, aka Yahuah T'Sebaoth, The Most High (TMH) from the Biblical description to an image of themselves. And following the lead of their father, Satan, they said,

> *"12 How art thou fallen from heaven, O Lucifer, son of the morning! How art thou cut down to the ground, which didst weaken the nations!*
>
> *13 For thou hast said in thine heart, I will ascend into heaven, I will exalt my throne above the stars of God: I will sit also upon the mount of the congregation, in the sides of the north:*
>
> *14 I will ascend above the heights of the clouds; I will be like The Most High.*
>
> *15 Yet thou shalt be brought down to hell, to the sides of the pit."*
>
> *Isaiah 14:12-15*

29

The first time we saw gentrification was not in a 'hood near you but rather in the Word of Yah. Now we have the wicked of the wicked tempting TMH by painting themselves in the image and likeness of Almighty Yahuah, His Son, and His people. This is what is meant by the Scripture that says,

> *"13 And the LORD God said unto the woman, What is this that thou hast done? And the woman said, The serpent beguiled me, and I did eat...*
>
> *15 And I will put enmity between thee and the woman, and between thy seed and her seed; it shall bruise thy head, and thou shalt bruise his heel."*

Genesis 3:13,15

So, if we do not understand anything else about this book, know that these same European people are enemies of the God of Abraham, Isaac, and Jacob. They are the "border of wickedness" spoken of in Malachi 1:4 and the seed of Satan.

Who else in their right mind would attempt to take on the Creator of the Universe in His own Universe that He created? Many have said that Nick Cannon and LeSean Jackson are anti-Semitic for quoting Hitler, but if what he was quoted as saying is true, then we have to ask who are these fools that think they can take on TMH, the Creator of all things, and win.

At this point, we have to figure out Who's Who, right? The Scripture is clear that there would be a people, who are the people, and there would be people who say they are the people? Let's see if we can figure it out.

Who does He look like? Who do we look like?

Heavenly Father, is that You?

L et's go back and look at the beginning again. God or Yahuah (in Paleo Hebrew) or The Most High Yah said in His Word,

> "In the beginning was the Word. The Word was with God and the Word was God."
>
> John 1:1
>
> When man was created, He said, "Let Us make man in Our IMAGE and after Our LIKENESS."
>
> Genesis 1:26
>
> And so He created man out of the DUST OF THE GROUND and breathed into him the Breath of Life."
>
> Genesis 2:7

The breath of life?

The breath of whose life?

The breath of God's Life.

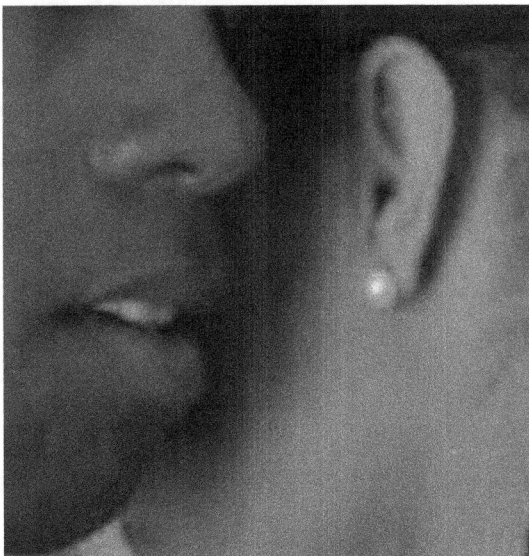

The Talk Game

We have established that man was given the breath of life from the Creator. Great! What has that got to do with what the Creator God looks like? If you are like most people, you have been told that we have no idea what God or any celestial being looks like as there is no description of Yahshua, aka Jesus Christ in Scripture. These folks generally say this with a picture of a white Jesus just out of focus over their shoulder. Imagine the talk game you have to tell people there is no description of Abba Yah or Yahshua in Scripture with a false image of Christ or ha'Maschiach in the background?

All this was possible because He said that Israel would be blinded,

> *"25 For I would not, brethren, that ye should be ignorant of this mystery, lest ye should be wise in your own conceits; that blindness in part is happened to Israel, until the fulness of the Gentiles be come in."*
>
> *Romans 11:25*

So, it's not their talk game that is strong but rather His talk game that rules. If Abba Yah says it will be, it will be no matter what you may say or think. There is no other way that anything could happen unless and until He says it will happen. The God, aka the Elohim of Abraham, Isaac, and Jacob controls every move on the chessboard. Besides Him, there is no one else,

> *"39 See now that I, even I, am He, and there is no god with Me: I kill, and I make alive; I wound, and I heal: neither is there any hat can deliver out of My hand."*
>
> *Deuteronomy 32:39*

Let's continue. Because Abba Yah, aka The Most High (TMH), said His people would be blinded until the time of the Gentiles has been fulfilled. You and I have read right past Scriptures that gave us descriptions of Heavenly beings. Now

34

that this veil has been lifted from our eyes, we can clearly see that there are multiple descriptions of Abba Yah in Scripture.

Let's begin with God the Father, aka Abba Yah Himself. Is there a description of Him in the Bible? I'm glad you asked.

> *"⁹ I beheld till the thrones were cast down, and the ANCIENT of DAYS did sit, whose garment was white as snow, and the hair of His head like the PURE WOOL: His throne was like the fiery flame, and His wheels as burning fire."*

> *Daniel 7:9*

So then there is a description of TMH's hair, at least, and it's like WOOL. Ever since the Gentiles have taken over the promulgation of the Word, we have read over this Scripture for hundreds of years without noticing that TMH describes exactly what He looks like. Well, at least His hair is described. But still, your talk game has got to be all hella strong to hide this in plain sight all this time. And our God has the strongest talk game around. Just imagine how strong TMH's talk game is to get you to say there is no description of Him in Scripture while describing Himself in Scripture? And don't forget that the same talk game is the same talk game that says, in the end, He is coming back for His bloodline people. It was and is that same talk game that delivered Daniel from the lions' den, Shadrach, Meschach, and Abednego from the fiery furnace, Goliath's head into the hand of David, and the life of the so-called Negro from the hand of the oppressors we face today.

35

But before we move on, let's pause right here and ask...
WHO ELSE ON EARTH HAS HAIR LIKE WOOL?

I will leave that right here. Let's continue.

Abba Yah's and His Talk Game

His talk game is better known as His Word,

"[11] So shall My Word be that goeth forth out of My mouth: it shall not return unto me void, but it shall accomplish that which I please, and it shall prosper in the thing whereto I sent it."

Isaiah 55:11

And,

"19 God is not a man, that he should lie; neither the son of man, that He should repent: hath He said, and shall He not do it? or hath He spoken, and shall He not make it good?"

Numbers 23:19

And then,

"1 God, who at sundry times and in divers manners spake in time past unto the fathers by the prophets,

2 Hath in these last days spoken unto us by His Son, whom He hath appointed Heir of all things, by whom also He made the worlds;

3 Who being the brightness of His glory, and the express image of His person, and upholding all things by the WORD OF HIS POWER, when He had by Himself purged our sins, sat down on the right hand of the Majesty on high;"

Hebrews 1:1-3

Now back to the lecture at hand. Abba Yah, aka TMH through John goes on to say,

> *"2 And immediately I was in the spirit: and, behold, a Throne was set in Heaven and One sat on the Throne.*
>
> *3 And He that sat was to look upon like a Jasper and a Sardine stone:"* Revelation 4:2-3

When we look at the two stones, we see they both are a dark reddish-brown color. So if TMH has woolly hair and dark skin, we MUST ask the question, "Who does He look like? Who do we look like?"

I'm just saying.

But what about the other part of the Godhead? Yahshua ha'Maschiach or the One most ignorantly called Jesus Christ? Is there a description of Him in Scripture? Let's take a look.

When we go back to the book of Revelation, we find this description,

> *"13 And in the midst of the seven candlesticks one like unto the Son of man, clothed with a garment down to the foot, and girt about the paps with a golden girdle.*
>
> *14 His head and His hairs were white LIKE WOOL, as white as snow; and His eyes were as a flame of fire;*
>
> *15 And His feet like unto fine brass, as if they burned in a furnace;..."*
>
> Revelation 1:13-15

38

Most of the European Gentiles will try to say that the "head... white like wool" proves that at least Yahshua had a white head. However, a closer look shows that in Strongs, the definition is "white, bright or brilliant." So the term white could actually mean bright or brilliant.

But let's not stop here. When you look even closer, you will notice that Strong's makes an extraordinary reference to the term "white" in the Book of Luke. When you follow the reference, it leads you to Luke,

> *"²⁹ And as He prayed, the fashion of His countenance was altered, and His raiment was WHITE AND GLISTERING."*
>
> *Luke 9:29*

The Greek term is nearly identical in both cases. Strong's again defines white as not just white in color but possibly bright or brilliant. So could it be that what was really being said was that Yahshua's head or countenance was bright and brilliant?

Let's go deeper. When we look for more descriptions of Abba Yah and Yahshua, we find this,

> *"⁵ Then I lifted up mine eyes, and looked, and behold a certain Man clothed in linen, whose loins were girded with fine gold of Uphaz:*
>
> *⁶ His body also was like the beryl, and His face as the appearance of lightning, and His eyes as lamps of fire, and His arms and His feet like in colour to polished brass, and the voice of His words like the voice of a multitude."*

39

Daniel 10:5-6

Notice once again the face is like lightening or brilliant, which is in line with Revelation 1:14.

Some say this is the description of Yahshua and others say it is the description of one of the chief angels. No matter which of these is correct, the point here is that his skin color is polished brass, which is dark brown. And His face or countenance is like the APPEARANCE OF LIGHTENING.

HEBREW ISRAELITE

BRASS   BURNT BRASS

So when we look at Scripture, we find that there is no instance that Abba Yah or Yahshua is described as having anything other than woolly hair and some variation of dark brown skin tone.

And, of course, we have the obligatory comment that these were all spiritual visions. The answer, of course, is... "AND?"

Anyone with two minutes of biblical understanding will tell you that EVERYTHING begins in the spirit realm, then comes to the natural realm. Therefore the spirit realm is more real than the natural realm. We know that to be true in our everyday lives. Consider the house you live in now; it began as a thought in someone's mind. The shoes you wear. The car you drive. No matter what we see in the world around us, it all started with a thought in someone's mind, which is in the spirit realm. Queue The Temptations "Just My Imagination."

So, the bottom line here is that TMH Yah is a Negro God. His Son came through a Negro people, which makes both Him and them Negroes.

> "9 Jesus saith unto him, Have I been so long time with you, and yet hast thou not known me, Philip? he that hath seen Me hath seen the Father; and how sayest thou then, Shew us the Father?"

> John 14:9

Yeah. I hear you. What's that you say? How does any of this prove that the God of all the Universe is a Negro God and that the children of Israel are a Black people?

Ok, so let's take it from the top one more time. Abba Yah says in Daniel 7:9 He has hair like PURE WOOL. In Revelation 4:2-3, He says the ONE seated on The Throne appears to be dark reddish-brown like Jasper and Sardine stones found in the Israelite Ephod pictures above. And His Son has virtually the same description.

41

Roll Tape

Now, for His Chosen people, you know in the hood, the first thing we do when somebody claims "he 'da daddy" is to ask who he looks like. Our Elohim even said that He would make man in His Image after His Likeness. He made His people to look like Him. Before we go to Maury, let's go to the videotape.

When first seen, the Hebrews were chilling in Canaan. The brothers were pissed that Joseph not only said his brothers would bow down to him, but they also knew he was Jacob's favorite son. So angry were his brothers that they sold him into slavery. Fast forward almost twenty years, and the brothers find themselves standing before this Egyptian dude that is dishing out the Egyptian equivalent of government cheese. However, one problem is that Joseph is their brother, but the brothers cannot tell the difference between Joseph and the rest of the Egyptians. You know all of you look alike to me,

"8 And Joseph knew his brethren, but they knew not him."

Genesis 42:8

A two-second scan of the myriad of Egyptian wall murals reveals that there isn't a single image of any white-looking Egyptians. Ahhh, they're all brothers. Say it ain't so Joe, say it ain't so. There has to be at least one white man, at least one, right? That would be a hard

"NO."

Fast forward to Moses. He was a Hebrew raised in Pharaoh's house. When he came of age, he killed an Egyptian for attacking one of his Hebrew brethren. Another Hebrew saw it and threatened to drop a dime on Moses. So Moses did what any self-respecting brother would do... he bounced.

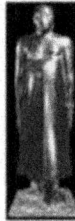

MOSES and EXODUS
source: british-israel.ca

The hieroglyph above, read from right to left reads M-S ZWAWZ-ims (Zravgones ="draw") which is Moshe, "Star Prince" (of Thebes)?

Today, the "Statue" of Moses above - in black diorite - is in the Museum of Art History in Vienna but the base and feet are in the National Museum of Ireland in Dublin.

After he made like a banana and split, he came across some damsels trying to water their father's animals. However, the male shepherds tried to run the damsels off, but Moses stepped in,

"¹⁷ And the shepherds came and drove them away: but Moses stood up and helped them, and watered their flock.

¹⁸ And when they came to Reuel their father, he said, How is it that ye are come so soon to day?

¹⁹ And they said, An EGYPTIAN delivered us out of the hand of the shepherds, and also drew water enough for us, and watered the flock."

Exodus 2:17-19

We're still looking for the first European or white Egyptian during Biblical times. So we know that when Moses took off and ran into these ladies, they couldn't tell the difference between Moses and a random Egyptian because he looked like the Egyptians who were an all BLACK people just like Moses.

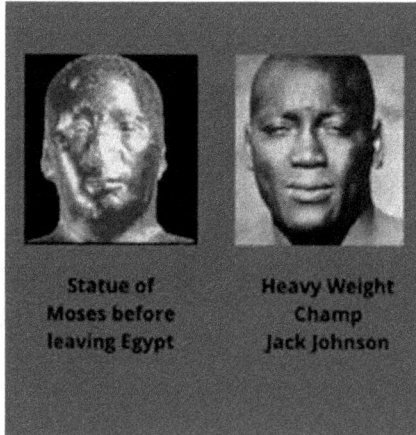

Statue of Moses before leaving Egypt

Heavy Weight Champ Jack Johnson

But let's not stop there. Let's move on to Paul. In Acts 21, we find that Paul was at Jerusalem for Pentecost. A fight breaks out because some Jews had seen him elsewhere appearing to bring Gentiles into the synagogue. The soldiers came to break it up and take Paul into custody. The officer assumed he was an Egyptian. And this is what he said,

> *"[37] And as Paul was to be led into the castle, he said unto the chief captain, May I speak unto thee? Who said, Canst thou speak Greek?*
>
> *[38] Art not thou that EGYPTIAN, which before these days madest an uproar, and leddest out into the wilderness four thousand men that were murderers?*
>
> *[39] But Paul said, I am a man which am a Jew of Tarsus, a city in Cilicia, a citizen of no mean city..."*

> *Acts 21:37-39*

We know that the Egyptians were a Black people (the word Egypt means black land or land of the blacks) and the Israelites were consistently confused with these same Black Africans for over two thousand years, then we know the Israelites were and are a Black people as well.

Zondervan's Bible Dictionary says it this way:

> *Ham... The youngest son of Noah... He became the progenitor of the dark races; not the Negroes, but the Egyptians, Ethiopians, Libyans, and Canaanites*

> *Gen. 10:6-20*

Who 'da People?

Now you know Massa ain't gonna take this lying down. Not after he has spent hundreds of years building brand fake white

45

Jesus in your mind with his silky white skin, ocean blue eyes, and straight blond hair. Not after all the millions spent on movies, books, and imaging disseminated worldwide to cement these false images in your mind.

If you think Massa will simply bow down and admit the truth, you got another thing coming. He will demand extraordinary proof of these claims. When he loses on that account, he will shout claims of racism. And when all else fails, he will simply say, "Why does it matter?"

We just started by proving from the Biblical text that we are actually 'da People. But what about the historical artifacts and the scientific?

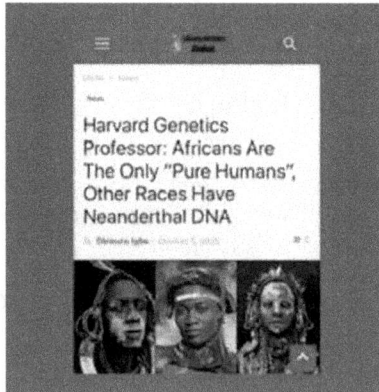

Harvard Genetics Professor: Africans Are The Only "Pure Humans", Other Races Have Neanderthal DNA

It is now a well-established fact that the first humans came out of Africa. In fact, scientists readily acknowledged that black folks are the ONLY 100% humans on the planet. That is,

46

of course, until we began to connect our blackness to our Biblical roots, and now, all of a sudden, we have new information (or lies) that says black folks also have Neanderthal and/or Denisovan DNA.

Fortunately, we no longer take our oppressors' word for it. Now we must look to the Scriptures for Biblical truth backed up by archeological evidence to determine who the true bloodline Israelites are today.

Study the Scriptures. When I was first saved, I went to a church that taught about God's promises and focused on the promises described in Deuteronomy 28, where Yah told us that if we obeyed Him, we would be blessed. They never discussed the second half that talked about the curses because they said the curses only applied to the Jews. Western European Style Christianity teaches that they get all the cake and ice cream and none of the castor oil or bitter medicine. So, like everyone else, I did not pay much attention to verses 15-68. Looking back on how we could be deceived into believing the bad things didn't belong to us but only the good things belong to us is beyond me.

The Pastor did a series about racism, and I couldn't help but wonder about the stark difference in reality for black folks versus white folks' experience with the gospel. White folks all seem to be experiencing the blessings that were promised even as they sinned as much as the biblical Hebrews or more, but black folks were still mired in poverty and lack.

This brought up a question in my spirit that I asked the Pastor about. How was it on Sunday morning as I rode from my cool crib at the beach in an all-white neighborhood to church in the 'hood that most of our people suffered poverty, sickness, and lack while serving God, I would see amazing blessings for my white neighbors? They worshipped at the altar of football at the sports bar or fun and sun at the beach. Meanwhile, when I got down to the 'hood for church it was all aglow with black folks making their way to church in broken-down neighborhoods living broken lives? Pastor did not have an answer, so all I could do was say, hmm… (a nod to Arsenio). But Pastor did ask the question, "Why do they hate us so much? What have we done?" KRS1 asked virtually the same question in his 90s rap tune, "Why Is That?" Then the Lord brought to my remembrance, "Because they have hated Me, they will hate you."

Breadcrumbs Please

But how does being hated make us the people? Good question. It's a start, but that cannot be the only way to tell who we are. The great thing about the God of Abraham, Isaac, and

Jacob is that He leaves little breadcrumbs along the way that you can use to find your way back to Him. The first little bread crumb is the recognition that things tend to repeat themselves with TMH Yah. After reading through the OT several times, I noticed that there is this pattern that continued to repeat itself over and over again. Abba Yah blesses us and gives us commands to keep. He warns us against sin that would remove His blessing from us. We sin against Abba Yah. Judgment falls on us. We repent and ask for His forgiveness of our transgression as a people. He forgives our sin. Then we come back to Him with a contrite heart. He blesses us, and the cycle begins again.

The next breadcrumb, Deuteronomy 28:1, tells us that if we harken to His voice and do all He has commanded us, then we would be blessed above all nations. And everything we set our hands to would be blessed,

> *"¹ And it shall come to pass, if thou shalt hearken diligently unto the voice of the LORD thy God, to observe and to do all His Commandments which I command thee this day, that the LORD thy God will set thee on high above all nations of the earth:*
>
> *² And all these blessings shall come on thee, and overtake thee, if thou shalt hearken unto the voice of the LORD thy God."*
>
> Deuteronomy 28:1-2

However, if we do not keep His Commandments, we would be cursed above all nations, as Deuteronomy 28:15 says. And we would be at the bottom in every nation,

"15 But it shall come to pass, if thou wilt not hearken unto the voice of the LORD thy God, to observe to do all His Commandments and His Statutes which I command thee this day; that all these curses shall come upon thee, and overtake thee:"

Deuteronomy 28:15

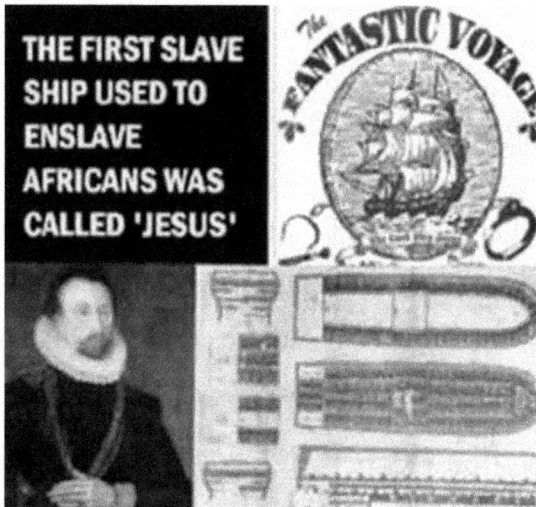

The Deuteronomy 28:68 Controversy

Then there is this breadcrumb,

"68 And the LORD shall bring thee into Egypt again with ships, by the way whereof I spake unto thee, thou shalt see it no more

again: and there ye shall be sold unto YOUR ENEMIES or bondmen and bondwomen, and no man shall buy you."

Deuteronomy 28:68

This is the Big Gun, the Granddaddy of them all, the pièce de résistance. The ONE Scripture that proves "We 'da People." The only problem is, many other Scriptures would bring us to the same conclusion. But let's break this one down.

First, Yah has the ability to swing back and forth between spiritual and physical metaphors within the same sentence. He is the Creator and can make that change anytime He wants. Thus, Egypt is a metaphor for the spirit behind the country that is called Mizraim or bondage. What is being said is this:

1. We would be taken back into Mizraim or bondage again, this time with ships.
2. We would not see the Promised Land again.
3. We would then be sold to our enemies.
4. No man would buy us or more precisely, redeem us as was the custom of the Hebrews of Biblical times.

First, there are ONLY one people that have been taken anywhere as slaves AS AN ENTIRE PEOPLE on ships. And that is the so-called Negro. More on this in a moment.

Second, the children of Israel were forced out of the Holy Land in 70AD and have not been back since. The people in the

Land today are Europeans posing as Israel the way Revelation 2:9 and 3:9 said they would, whose ancestors are the sons of Japheth. Again, this will be covered in a later chapter.

The third point about being sold to our enemies must be noted. If Abba Yah says that someone is my enemy, then if I know what's good for me, I better take Him at His Word. Who were we sold to? Europeans, Arabs, Asians, East Indians, Native Americans, and Africans. The truth is that we have been sold to every nation of people and that the whole of the world economy is built on the backs of Negro Hebrew slaves. No matter who the people are, we have been sold to them to be their slaves. This caused Jeremiah to ask Abba Yah,

> *"14 Is Israel a servant? Is he a homeborn slave? why is he spoiled?"*

> *Jeremiah 2:14*

We are the only people who have been enslaved by every nation and have never been paid by anybody for our labor. Not to worry, though, the entire world will be our servants in the next dispensation. According to Scripture, every nation will serve us or be destroyed,

> *"12 For the nation and kingdom that will not serve thee shall perish; yea, those nations shall be utterly wasted."*

> *Isaiah 60:12*

Reparations are not on the menu for you, Black man, aka Israel, because TMH Yah has a better deal for those of our people that will forsake Babylon and return to His laws, statutes, and commands. The entire world economy will be brought to you, Black man, and laid at your feet. Sadly, two-thirds of our people will reject the better deal Abba Yah has for us so that they can continue to follow fake white Jesus, aka Cesare Borgia and the Black Pastors, aka false prophets that continue to promote a people who are the seed of Satan along with fake jakes and pagan worship practices.

This last point about no one buying us is confusing until you realize that in the Hebrew culture, when a family member is in debt and at risk of being enslaved to pay off debts, the next of kin has the right and responsibility to buy out the relative's debts to keep them from being sold into bondage. This person is known as the Kinsman Redeemer,

> "25 If thy brother be waxen poor, and hath sold away some of his possession, and if any of his kin come to redeem it, then shall he redeem that which his brother sold."
>
> Leviticus 25:25 (also see Book of Ruth).

The Scripture tells us that Yahshua ha'Maschiach has been sent to 'redeem us from the curse of the Law.' The Scripture also says,

> *"3 For thus saith the LORD, Ye have sold yourselves for naught; and ye shall be redeemed without money."*

Isaiah 52:3

The Scripture then says that,

> *"28 Even as the Son of man came not to be ministered unto, but to minister, and to give His life a ransom for many."*

Matthew 20:28

Yahshua ha'Maschiach, whom many ignorantly call Jesus, is our Kinsman Redeemer who bought us back NOT with money but with His own blood.

Calling Fire Down on Our Heads

When the Hebrews were last seen in Scripture, they were being spread abroad into all nations after having rejected Yahshua as Messiah and famously saying,

> *"22 Pilate saith unto them, What shall I do then with Jesus which is called Christ? They all say unto him, Let Him be crucified...*
>
> *25Then answered all the people, and said, His blood be on us, and on our children."*

Matthew 27:22, 25

We've been catching hell ever since. But wait, there are more breadcrumbs. Let's continue to see if some other Scriptural references or breadcrumbs would point to the so-called Black man or Negro being the Chosen seed of Israel. Before Yahshua was crucified, He made this prophetic utterance,

"23 But woe unto them that are with child, and to them that give suck, in those days! for there shall be great distress in the land, and wrath upon THIS PEOPLE.

24 And THEY shall fall by the edge of the sword, and SHALL BE LED AWAY CAPTIVE INTO ALL NATIONS: and Jerusalem shall be trodden down of the Gentiles, until the times of the Gentiles be fulfilled."
Luke 21:23-24

Okay, so who are THESE PEOPLE and THEY that are being spoken of in this passage? Well, when Jesus or Yahshua walked the earth, who was He living amongst? Since He was living in the Land of Israel, we know He was living amongst people known then as the Tribe of Judah or Yahuda as the ten Northern

Tribes were no longer in Israel. Of course, we know He was, in fact, a Jew or Yahudeen from the line of David.

But wait, what about this part about being led away captive into all nations? Every people or group has been enslaved at some point, so there is no way to tell who fits this prophecy, right?

Wrong.

Since the resurrection of ha'Maschiach, only one group of people fit this description, and it is the so-called Black man or Negro. Yes, just about every people or group has been enslaved. However, ONLY ONE PEOPLE have been enslaved as an entire people or group (man, woman, and child) throughout the world, and that is you, Black man, aka Negro, Israelite, or Hebrew. Our people have been in captivity in:

- North America
- South America
- The Islands
- Africa
- Europe
- The Middle East
- India
- Sri Lanka

- Indonesia
- China
- Japan
- Australia

All nations of people in the world have had Black, aka Negro people, as slaves. The European Slave Trade covered Europe and the Western Hemisphere, while the Arab Slave Trade covered the Middle East, Asia, and Australia. The people operating the Slave Trade are different, but the slaves were and are the same people.

Where Y'all From?

C'mon man, y'all Negroes be trippin', everybody knows the Jews ain't Black.

Yeah, that's what we've been told by Western European Style Christianity, Hollywood, and the Government all day, every day. This beast system tells us that God, Jesus, aka Yahshua, and the Chosen people are all white everywhere we turn. They say it so much with words and images that it must be true, and we must accept the propaganda, right? No. Not today, Satan. Not today. We're about to blow this up. Let's get it.

This entire topic will be covered in detail in the upcoming follow-up book that goes into a more complete Biblical,

Archeological, Scientific, and Genetic study. But today we're going to give you the twenty-five-cent tour. The Scripture says,

The Khazar kingdom in the early 10th century
Copyright ©2004 by Kevin A. Brook

"⁹ I know thy works, and tribulation, and poverty, (but thou art rich) and I know the blasphemy of them which say they are Jews, and are not, but are the synagogue of Satan."

Revelation 2:9

Yahshua tells us there are people who say they are Jews but are not. And are willing to blaspheme the God of all Creation in order to make this claim. They are willing to join themselves together with Satan against The Most High Yah in order to claim for themselves a covenant right that does not belong to them. These people, whoever they are, have decided to cast their lot in with Satan. Let's be clear, you are about to get your dome cracked lest ye repent, acknowledge, and bow before the so-called Negro, aka Hebrew Israelites. We know, of course, that

59

this will never happen until the Son of TMH Yah cracks the sky and cracks your cranium and forces you to bow before His people along with your king, who is none other than Satan.

So who are these people? Let's begin the tour. It turns out that there was a kingdom nestled between the Black Sea and the Caspian Sea just above the country of Georgia. The kingdom was called Khazaria. These people were a warlike people who were initially pagans. In the eighth century, they were being pressed by Christians, aka Roman Catholics on one side, and the Muslims from the east.

Their king at the time was Kagan Bulan. There was pressure on him to convert to either Christianity or Islam. He decided to convene a meeting of the two religions to see which was better. He noticed that both religious representatives referred to Abraham and the Hebrews in a favorable light. Wishing to remain independent and agreeable with both religions, King Bulan decided to embrace Judaism. Eventually, they sent for Talmudic rabbis to teach the new religion to the King's court.

In the end, this Khazarian kingdom was destroyed and dispersed by the Huns. Those not killed migrated west into Eastern Europe, where they became known as Jews. Most European historians try to pretend that there is no connection between Khazars and the European Jews so as to hide the fact that the jews are converts and, therefore, not true bloodline descendants of Abraham, Isaac, and Jacob.

> *"Many reference and historical sources have unequivocally identified that the bulk of the Ashkenazi Jews were derived from a people known as Khazars (or Chazars in some texts). The original Jewish Encyclopedia of 1905 revealed that the main stock of the Jews came from these Asiatic people known as Chazars or Khazars:"*
>
> *- Charles A. Weisman, Who is Esau-Edom, Weisman Publicans 1991, pg 9.*

In Europe, there were at least three distinct sets of Hebrews.

The Ashkenazi converts, the Sephardic converts from the Hyrcanus era, and the true bloodline Yahudeen or Judeans that ruled with the Moors when they came up from North Africa.

According to an excerpt from John Ogilby's book, Africa, being an Accurate Description of the Regions..., the true Hebrews began to be kicked out of one country after another, starting with Italy in 1350AD until finally in 1492AD they were kicked out of Spain just as Columbus was leaving for the New World in search of the Lost Tribes that he found on his fourth voyage that took him down to South America where he found the people he was looking for. Now that the true Hebrews had been removed from the scene and deported to West Africa to an area that eventually was named Negroland, the converts could begin claiming they were the actual bloodline Jews from Scripture. Nothing could be further from the truth.

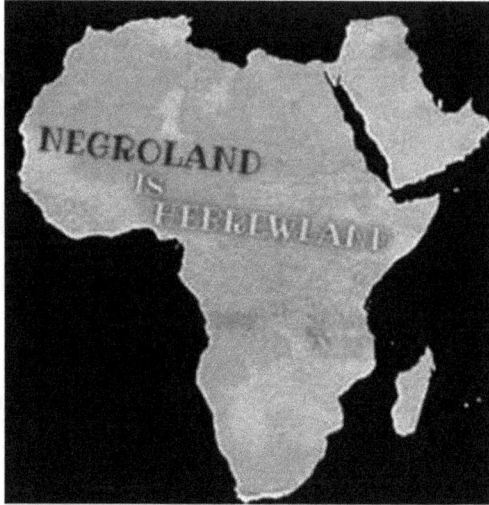

Negro, Nigger, and NEGROLAND

While in Spain and Portugal, our people began to be referred to as not just Judeans or Yahudeen but also as Negroes. Where did this name come from? Many of us have wondered where the name came from and how we got it. For the answer to that, we must turn to our preeminent researcher for all things Hebrew in Europe, Benayah Ben Israel. His research reveals that originally the name Negro came about due to one of our ancestors named YahYa, born in about 1050AD. He was a warrior on the level of King David. He fought alongside King Alfonso and was so highly decorated that the king gave him an area of the country called "Aldeia dos Negros" or Two Villages of the Negroes. Whereupon they added the name Negro to their name. Yahya and his descendants became known as the Negroes by the Portuguese people. One of his descendants became the chief Rabbi in Lisbon, where many of the people from the Village of Negroes migrated. From Lisbon, most of the Hebrews were deported to West Africa.

In John Ogilby's book, he referenced the fact that Hebrews that were deported from Portugal as part of "The Inquisition" ended up in great numbers on both sides of the Niger River. These Hebrews, along with others that had migrated to the area after the fall of Jerusalem in 70AD were given the name Nigger because of the area they inhabited around the Niger River. It is important to note that the name Niger was originally pronounced NIGGER. The pronunciation was later updated to hide the fact that we came from this area.

When you look at any one of Africa's maps created back during the Middle Ages, you find they all had an area curiously named Negroland. Of course, as more and more Black folks started to read, the Europeans did what they always do and removed the identifiers in hopes that we wouldn't notice. And for several hundred years, we didn't notice because as Paul said under the unction of the Holy Spirit or Ruach ha'Kodesh,

> *"25 For I would not, brethren, that ye should be ignorant of this mystery, lest ye should be wise in your own conceits; that blindness in part is happened to Israel, until the fulness of the Gentiles be come in."*
>
> *Romans 11:25*

Uh oh, if we are not blind anymore, then the Gentiles' fullness has come in and it's game over for you Gentiles. Now is the time for you to turn to Isaiah 14:1-2 so you can see what your fate is IF you cleave to Israel, aka the so-called Negro. And that is for those that bow. For the rest of you hanging on to that pagan homosexual false messiah pushed by the Western European Style Christian Church, it's curtains. Death and destruction for sure.

One of the really curious things about Negroland is that the inhabitants of the land had another name for it. They called it Êʋê Nyigba or Hebrewland. So Negroland is really Hebrewland.

All of these have been hidden from us because if we were allowed to research, someone would eventually ask where that name Negroland came from, which tracks back to the Negroes and would then track back to Portugal, Spain, and the Inquisition. Which would then track back to the fact that expulsion of the Hebrews from the various European nations was about kicking these Black Judeans or Yahudeen out of Europe. This will expose the fact that in Europe, there were different sets of Jews. The true bloodline Yahudeen, the converted white European Jews, and the Sephardim converts from John Hyrcanus. Consequently, this will cause any rational thinking person to connect Revelation 2:9, 3:9, and Ezekiel 36:5 to the imposters living in the Land today.

Greatest Identity Theft of All Time

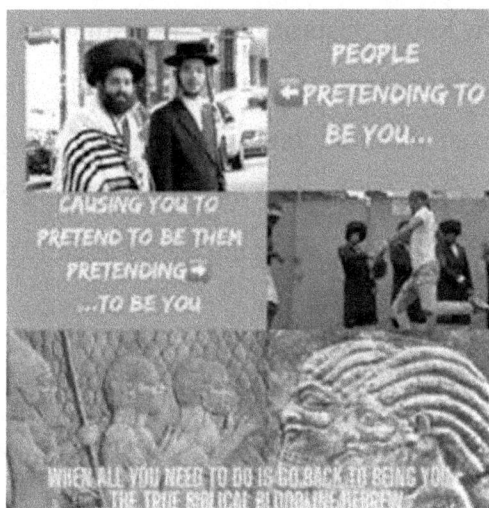

Back to the Khazarians. About one hundred years after King Bulan converted His people to Judaism, one of the chief Spanish Rabbis heard about this Israelite state in the north. Upon hearing about this large Hebrew state, Rabbi Hasdai ibn Shaprut reached out to the king of Khazaria at the time, King Joseph. The Rabbi asked how a large Hebrew state could exist without anyone knowing about it. He also asked about his lineage, to which King Joseph responded, "Of what people, of what family, and of what tribe are you? Know that we descended from Japheth, through his son Togarmah. I have found in the genealogical books of my ancestors that Togarmah had ten sons..."

King Joseph's Letter to Rabbi Shaprut

Even with Rabbi Shaprut, it is interesting that he does not identify himself as being of the line of Jacob, which means he was perhaps an Edomite Jew or Sephardic Jew (these were people brought into the land by the Assyrian King, Shalmaneser to replace the Yahudeen or Judah, see 2 Kings 17). In his letter to King Joseph, the Rabbi defines his lineage as,

> *"I, Hasdai, son of Isaac, son of Ezra, belonging to the exiled Jews of Jerusalem in Sepharad, a servant of my lord the King, bow to the earth before him and prostrate myself towards the abode of your Majesty from a distant land..."*

> *- Rabbi Hasdai ibn Shaprut's letter to King Joseph*

In Medieval times, everyone understood that these white Jews were converts and that the black bloodline Yahudeen who

66

had migrated into Europe with the Moors and for about 800 years ruled Ireland, Scotland, and Britain were the true Israel. It wasn't until The Inquisition that the imposter Jews or converts began to assert themselves as true Israel when true Israel was deported to Africa.

These converted Jews also seem to have some Edomite lineage that they used to assert themselves as true Israel. Because of the John Hyrcanus forced conversions, these imposters had some knowledge and understanding of the culture. As we know from Scripture, Edom was conquered by Rome and mixed in with the Romans. Because the Edomites were absorbed into Rome and freely intermingled into Roman society, many looked white just like any other European. Even their own people acknowledge this in their writings about who they are and where they came from,

> "...the large majority of surviving Jews in the world is of Eastern European, and thus perhaps mainly of Khazar---origin. If so, this would mean that their ancestors came not from the Jordan but from the Volga, not from Canaan, but from the Caucasus; ...and that genetically they are more closely related to the Hun, Uigur, and Magyar tribes than to the seed of Abraham, Isaac, and Jacob."
>
> - Arthur Koestler, The Thirteenth Tribe, Random House 1967, pg. 17

Historian H. G. Wells stated,

"...the Idumeans (Edomites) were. . . made Jews, . . and a Turkish people (Khazars) were mainly Jews in South Russia. The main part of Jewry never was in Judea and had never come out of Judea."

- HG Wells, The Outline of History, 3rd Ed, The MacMillian Company 1922, pg 494

The funny thing about TMH, though, is that He leaves these breadcrumbs for His people to find their way home and expose the workers of iniquity. So let's look at another one of those breadcrumbs. The first breadcrumb here is in their name. The imposter jews call themselves Ashkenazi Jews. A simple two-minute search of the Bible and Google proves that these people are not within the bloodline of the Biblical Hebrews.

"2 The sons of Japheth; Gomer, and Magog, and Madai, and Javan, and Tubal, and Meshech, and Tiras.

3 And the sons of Gomer; ASHKENAZ, and Riphath, and Togarmah.

4 And the sons of Javan; Elishah, and Tarshish, KITTIM, and Dodanim.

5 By these were the isles of the Gentiles divided in their lands; every one after his tongue, after their families, in their nations."

Genesis 10:1-5

So we see in verse 3 that Ashkenaz is the grandson of Japheth. In order to be a bloodline Hebrew, then Ashkenaz would need to be in Shem's bloodline. This in and of itself disqualifies Ashkenazi from being true Israel. They will try to claim that they innocently picked up this surname when they moved into the area. Since they were welcomed into the area, there would be no reason to change their name, which King Joseph of Khazaria already confirmed.

It has always been interesting to note that the Ashkenazi Jews have never called themselves Shemites but rather Semites. When you have a heritage that links back to Abba Yah's Chosen people, you would think that this would be something to hold on to as tightly as possible.

Speaking in Tongues

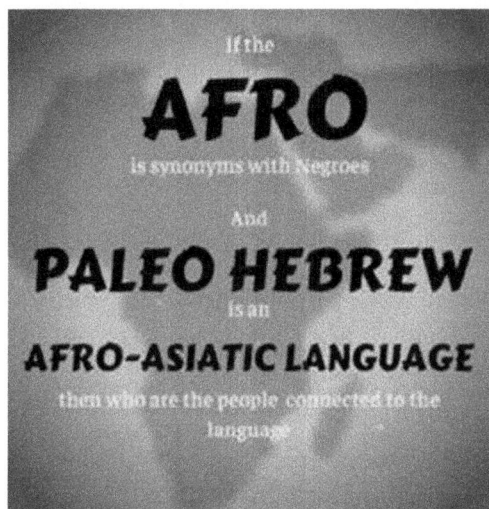

Then there is the matter of the language itself. Hebrew falls within the AFRO-ASIATIC Language group. WAIT. HOL(d-the "d" is silent in the 'hood) UP. STOP. Full pause. Say what now?

Paleo Hebrew is an Afro-Asiatic Language? Yes. AFRO-ASIATIC. What does that mean? It means exactly what it sounds like. Oxford Dictionary definition is as follows:

AFRO - a thick hairstyle consisting of very tight curls that sticks out all around the head, like the natural hair of some black people.

As a prefix - a combining form of Africa: Afro-American; Afro- Asiatic. Also, especially before a vowel, Afro-.

Uhhh, wait. Are you trying to say Hebrew is an African or black language?

Yes...

How do we know? We need to look no further than the region where Afro-Asiatic languages are spoken. Africa! In much of sub- Saharan Africa, you find the Israelites. Here we find ALL of the Tribes. Not one or two but ALL of them. As pointed out in the book by John Ogilby and many other European scholars, there are Hebrew Tribes all over sub-Saharan. In Allen Godbey's book, "The Lost Tribes Myth," there is a map of Africa pointing out many places where Hebrew Israelites can be found. This, of course, validates the scholarship of Rudolph R. Windsor's book "From Babylon to Timbuktu," which points out that up to one million Hebrews escaped from Roman destruction in 70AD by going down into Africa. A place our forefathers always went when fleeing persecution.

When studying our people's languages in Africa, we find similarities across all their languages, with most of the differences being in dialect. Many of their words and customs agree with Scripture. Most of the countries end in some version of Yah like Nigeria, Ghana, Liberia, Kenya, etc. And we know that Yah is a name for our Elohim Yahuah. In the Scripture, He said,

> *"14 If My people, which are called by My name, shall humble themselves, and pray, and seek My face, and turn from their wicked ways; then will I hear from heaven, and will forgive their sin, and will heal their land."*

> *2 Chronicles 7:14*

And so these Black folks, aka Hebrew, have the Father's name in everything they do. When looking at many of the slaves' manifests, it is apparent that most of the names have the sound of "Abba Yah" in their name. It's in our DNA. Even in those ghetto names given to our children, we find the name of our God buried in our Elohim:

- Elijah

- D'Asia
- Isaiah
- Joshua
- Josiah
- Kesha
- Nakeesha

Hebrew is an Afro-Asiatic language spoken by Afro-Asiatic Black people. It's a land with a people who have Afro-style hair, clothes, and lifestyle who serve a God that says He has the same woolly hair and dark reddish-brown skin like the people he created in His image and after His likeness.

Can the Imposters Do That?

Before moving to the Holy Land, the European Jews spoke Yiddish, not Paleo Hebrew. The difference between Yiddish and Hebrew is defined this way,

"Hebrew is a Semitic language (a subgroup of the Afro-Asiatic languages, languages spoken across the Middle East), while Yiddish is a German dialect which integrates many languages, including German, Hebrew, Aramaic, and various Slavic and Romance languages."

Schools had to be opened to teach the arriving Ashkenazim converts how to speak actual Hebrew, led by language revivalists like Eliezer Ben-Yehuda, who spent much of his life trying to revive the Hebrew language to replace Yiddish spoken by European jews with what some have called a modern twist.

Others like the notable German linguist Gotthelf Bergsträsser felt that Modern Hebrew was,

> *"in reality... a European language in transparent Hebrew disguise, with outwardly general European traits and individual language peculiarities, but with only totally superficial Hebrew character." Introduction to Semitic Languages ..." GotthelfBergsträßer (1928: 47)*

Ben-Yehuda tried to reverse engineer Yiddish into Modern Hebrew, which was a good effort, but at the end of the day, any honest linguist can immediately see that the effort fell woefully short. So, the next best thing is to run it up the flag pole, salute it, and tell the world it's a miracle of modern ingenuity and grit. And pretend that no one will notice if you maintain the deception long enough. The same way George Aiken advised Nixon to "claim victory and leave" in Vietnam and many in the Bush Administration advised him to do it in Iraq. They hope no one of consequence will notice. Except the only one of any consequence did notice and called them out thousands of years before the dirty deed.

How can that be? Everyone knows the Jews are white, Caucasian, European. There is no way the Jews are black. What about The Ten Commandments movie or Jesus Christ images we see everywhere or The Ben Hur movie or every Bible story, book, or movie I have ever seen? This simply cannot be true. It just can't be true.

Sorry to burst your bubble, but you've been lied to. TMH even told you more than twenty-five hundred years ago that you were going to be lied to,

> *"19 O LORD, my strength, and my fortress, and my refuge in the day of affliction, the Gentiles shall come unto thee from the ends of the earth, and shall say, surely our fathers have inherited lies, vanity, and things wherein there is no profit."*

> *Jeremiah 16:19*

When you read further up in this prophecy, TMH tells us that He will hunt the liars down and pay them double for what they have done to His Land and His people. So if you have any Gentile friends, you may want to warn them of that which is to come.

But that's not all. The Ashkenazi have known and admitted all along that they are not bloodline Israel. They admit this very fact in their own writings,

> *"Strictly speaking, it is incorrect to call an Ancient Israelite a 'Jew' or to call a contemporary Jew an Israelite or a Hebrew."*

Malak Yesha'Yahu ben Yahudah

1980 Jewish Almanac, p. 3

So, there you have it, sports fans, straight from the horses' mouth. They know they are not true bloodline Israel. They know, and now you know. Somebody queue Juicy by Biggie,

"It was all a dream.

I used to read Word Up Magazine.

Fake jakes and fake prophets all up in the limousine.

Images of fake white Jesus all up on my wall.

Christians trynna stop me from keepin' the Law."

Ok, so we took a few artistic liberties, but you get the point. Let's close out this section with a word from TMH,

> "[5] Therefore thus saith the Lord GOD; Surely in the fire of My jealousy have I spoken against the residue of the heathen, and against all Idumea, which have appointed My land into their possession with the joy of all their heart, with despiteful minds, to cast it out for a prey."
>
> Ezekiel 36:5

The God of the Hebrews, aka Israelites, the so-called Negroes called the end from the beginning. So now whatchu gonna do Negro, aka Israel? You gonna shoot or you gonna dibble? You gonna shoot and ride with TMH by repenting and coming back to His Laws, Statutes, and Commands? Wherein lies your power to tread over serpents, scorpions, and all of the

75

demonic power of your enemy, the European oppressors, fake jakes, and all that side with and conspire with them? Or you gonna dribble and stick with fake white Jesus, the pagan worship that comes with it, and the imposters sent to deceive you into following Satan into the Lake of Fire? And continue a life of bondage and servitude only to be destroyed in the end, just like those Israelites that refused to follow Moses and TMH Yah in the first Exodus?

White folks in America say, remember the Alamo. Black folks, aka Israel, better remember the Exodus,

> *"36 And God sent darkness upon Egypt, that the whole land of Egypt and Pathros became dark for three days, so that a man could not see his hand when he lifted it to his mouth.*
>
> *37 At that time died many of the people of Israel who had rebelled against the Lord and who would not hearken to Moses and Aaron, and believed not in them that God had sent them.*
>
> *38 And who had said, We will not go forth from Egypt lest we perish with hunger in a desolate wilderness, and who would not hearken to the voice of Moses.*
>
> *39 And the Lord plagued them in the three days of darkness, and the Israelites buried them in those days, without the Egyptians knowing of them or rejoicing over them."*
>
> *Book of Jasher 80:36-39*

The Bottom Line

According to Scripture, the end of the matter is this, ABBA YAH has a people and Satan has a people,

> *"15 And I will put enmity between thee and the woman, and between thy seed and her seed; it shall bruise thy head, and thou shalt bruise his heel."*

> *Genesis 3:15*

Abba Yah's people are made in His image and are like Him. The Black man who has been carried away captive into all nations with slave ships as Genesis 15:13, Luke 21:23-24, and Deuteronomy 28:68 say are indeed the true Hebrew Israelites spoken of in Scripture. We are the ones He is coming back to save along with the Gentiles and heathens that forsake their false God of Jesus Christ created by Constantine in 325AD and then cleave in submission to us as the Scripture has said in Isaiah 14:1-2.

Our Elohim reigns in righteousness and truth. Not lies and deception. And He clearly says,

> *"24 God is a Spirit: and they that worship Him must worship Him in spirit and in truth."*

> *John 4:24*

Liars and thieves need not apply.

Satan has a people that will join with him in attempting to overthrow the kingdom of Yah. As Satan has said,

"¹³ For thou hast said in thine heart, I will ascend into heaven, I will exalt my throne above the stars of God: I will sit also upon the mount of the congregation, in the sides of the north:

¹⁴ I will ascend above the heights of the clouds; I will be like the most High."

Isaiah 14:13-14

To which TMH responded,

"¹⁵ Yet thou shalt be brought down to hell, to the sides of the pit.

¹⁶ They that see thee shall narrowly look upon thee, and consider thee, saying, Is this the man that made the earth to tremble, that did shake kingdoms;

¹⁷ That made the world as a wilderness, and destroyed the cities thereof; that opened not the house of his prisoners?

¹⁸ All the kings of the nations, even all of them, lie in glory, everyone in his own house.

¹⁹ But thou art cast out of thy grave like an abominable branch, and as the raiment of those that are slain, thrust through with a sword, that go down to the stones of the pit; as a carcase trodden under feet.

²⁰ Thou shalt not be joined with them in burial, because thou hast destroyed thy land, and slain thy people: the seed of evildoers shall never be renowned.

²¹ Prepare slaughter for his children for the iniquity of their fathers; that they do not rise, nor possess the land, nor fill the face of the world with cities.

²² For I will rise up against them, saith the LORD of hosts, and cut off from Babylon the name, and remnant, and son, and nephew, saith the LORD.

²³ I will also make it a possession for the bittern, and pools of water: and I will sweep it with the besom of destruction, saith the LORD of hosts."

Malak Yesha'Yahu ben Yahudah

Isaiah 14:15-23

Our Kinsman Redeemer, Yahshua ha'Maschiach has said,

"9 Behold, I will make them of the synagogue of Satan, which say they are Jews, and are not, but do lie; behold, I will make them to come and worship before thy feet, and to know that I have loved thee."

Revelation 3:9

Y'all followers of fake white Jesus and Satan's imposter people are about to get this work. As for you, Black man, aka Israelites, aka Hebrews, get in the house. Get back to His laws, statutes, and commands wherein there are power and safety,

"10 Because thou hast kept the word of My patience, I also will thee from the hour of temptation, which shall come upon all the world, to try them that dwell upon the earth.

11 Behold, I come quickly: hold that fast which thou hast, that no man take thy crown.

12 Him that overcometh will I make a pillar in the temple of My God, and he shall go no more out: and I will write upon him the name of My God, and the name of the city of My God, which is new Jerusalem, which cometh down out of heaven from My God: and I will write upon him My new name.

13 He that hath an ear, let him hear what the Spirit saith unto the churches.

Revelation 3:10-13

Why Does It Matter?

The Seed of Satan

Abba Yah tells us that there is an ancient hatred that goes back to the beginning, back to the Garden where the serpent beguiled Eve into taking a bite of the forbidden fruit from the tree of the knowledge of good and evil. TMH Yah said to the serpent,

> *"15 And I will put enmity between thee and the woman, and between thy seed and her seed; it shall bruise thy head, and thou shalt bruise his heel."*
>
> *Genesis 3:15*

Malak Yesha'Yahu ben Yahudah

This prophecy foretells the struggle that will continue from the beginning to the end. It speaks of the overarching theme of Scripture. Abba Yah has a seed in the earth, and Satan has a seed in the earth realm as well. From the beginning of man's time here on earth, the two seeds have been waring against each other. Abba Yah or The Most High (TMH) said,

> *"¹ Moreover the word of the LORD came unto me, saying,*
>
> *² Son of man, set thy face against mount Seir, and prophesy against it,*
>
> *³ And say unto it, Thus saith the Lord GOD; Behold, O mount Seir, I am against thee, and I will stretch out mine hand against thee, and I will make thee most desolate.*
>
> *⁴ I will lay thy cities waste, and thou shalt be desolate, and thou shalt know that I am the LORD.*
>
> *⁵ Because thou hast had a perpetual hatred, and hast shed the blood of the children of Israel by the force of the sword in the time of their calamity, in the time that their iniquity had an end:*
>
> *⁶ Therefore, as I live, saith the Lord GOD, I will prepare thee unto blood, and blood shall pursue thee: sith thou hast not hated blood, even blood shall pursue thee.*
>
> *⁷ Thus will I make mount Seir most desolate, and cut off from it him that passeth out and him that returneth.*
>
> *⁸ And I will fill his mountains with his slain men: in thy hills, and in thy valleys, and in all thy rivers, shall they fall that are slain with the sword.*
>
> *⁹ I will make thee perpetual desolations, and thy cities shall not return: and ye shall know that I am the LORD."*
>
> *Ezekiel 35:1-9*

So then Satan has a seed, and the woman has a seed. Some would argue that the woman's seed, in this case, could have both a spiritual and physical meaning. Spiritually, the woman's seed means Israel, and physically, it means the seed planted in her by the man. For those that have an ear to hear, let them hear and understand.

Just like you cannot understand mathematics without being taught by a mathematician, you cannot understand the Scripture fully without the people to whom Abba Yah gave His Scripture, which are the Negroes, aka Israelites, Hebrews,

> "*3 For I could wish that myself were accursed from Christ for my brethren, my kinsmen according to the flesh:*
>
> *4 Who are Israelites; to whom pertaineth the adoption, and the glory, and the Covenants, and the giving of the Law, and the service of God, and the promises;*
>
> *5 Whose are the fathers, and of whom as concerning the flesh Christ came, who is over all, God blessed forever. Amen."*
>
> *Romans 9:3-5*

The Constantine Hijack

True Hebraic understanding has been hijacked first by the Roman Catholic Church beginning in 325AD with Constantine's Council of Nicaea. That changed our worship day from the Sabbath to Sunday and gave us Christmas and Easter Holidays instead of Abba Yah's Feast Days. And then extended by the Catholic Church's Dum Diversas in 1452 that authorized European nations to perpetually enslave non-Catholics, aka Negroes. This was the European or white religion of the day, both Judaism and Islam were considered religions of black people back then. As nearly ALL of the images of people who practiced these religions back then were of black people.

Original
Arabs

Original
Hebrews

In Africa which includes the so called Middle East the original inhabitants were ALL Black. Thus the original Arabs and Hebrews were black skinned people.

Later, it morphed into Western European Style Christianity due to the split between their church fathers. This movement was led by Martin Luther, whose only beef with the Catholic Church was their selling of indulgences to the common people. The only thing Martin Luther addressed in his 95 Thesis was indulgences, not the slavery hoisted upon the Hebrews. In fact, it is said that Martin Luther actually hated the Hebrews.

And then the European Ashkenazi jews hijacked our identity after we were deported from Spain and Portugal during The Inquisition and sent to West Africa. Most of these same imposter people claiming to be true Israel never set a foot inside the Holy Land before 1948. As we know, Abba Yah allowed all of this to happen because we left off the keeping of His Laws, Statutes, and Commands so that we could bow down to the false gods of wood (Western European Christianity) and stone (Islam). And just as Abba Yah said, they would use and abuse us. He allowed these people to take our heritage and be blessed for a short time so that we would be driven to jealousy. Meanwhile, we watched not from the sideline but the slave quarters while these people that will be our servants in the next dispensation lived like kings on our inheritance and made us into errand boys and bed wenches for their enjoyment.

If you are European, Arab, and Asian, none of our plights matters to you. However, if you are a child of Abraham, Isaac, and Jacob, this issue should matter to you more than anything else. Our God has said,

> *"8 And the LORD, He it is that doth go before thee; He will be with thee, He will not fail thee, neither forsake thee: fear not, neither be dismayed."*

Deuteronomy 31:8

We know that Abba Yah has His Word, His ha'Maschiach or Christ, and His Chosen people. Since Satan is not a creator and only has the ability to mimic our Elohim, he has his anti-Christ and His Chosen people. Because of our disobedience, Satan has been able to trick the world into accepting his false version of who is who. From the beginning, there has always been a description of our Elohim, His ha'Maschiach, and His people in Scripture. The trick of the devil is always to get you to

85

doubt what you know to be true. Once he gets you to doubt, he then is able to deceive you into cursing yourself.

As an example, when Eve ate the forbidden fruit, he was able to cause her to fall not by force but by deception,

> *"16 And the LORD God commanded the man, saying, Of every tree of the garden thou mayest freely eat:*
>
> *17 But of the tree of the knowledge of good and evil, thou shalt not eat of it: for in the day that thou eatest thereof thou shalt surely die."*

Genesis 2:16-17

Adam was commanded not to eat of the forbidden fruit. However, what he must have told Eve was slightly different,

> *"1 Now the serpent was more subtle than any beast of the field which the LORD God had made. And he said unto the woman, Yea, hath God said, Ye shall not eat of every tree of the garden?*
>
> *2 And the woman said unto the serpent, We may eat of the fruit of the trees of the garden:*
>
> *3 But of the fruit of the tree which is in the midst of the garden, God hath said, Ye shall not eat of it, neither shall ye touch it, lest ye die.*
>
> *4 And the serpent said unto the woman, Ye shall not surely die:"*
>
> *Genesis 3:1-4*

Abba Yah did not say, don't touch the fruit. He told Adam, don't eat the fruit. So Satan was able to exploit this small opening and cause all of mankind to fall. The weapon of the enemy is deception. Using this same ability to deceive, our enemy has misled the world into believing that Abba Yah is white, Jesus is white, and the true Hebrew Israelites are white. In fact, it is Satan, the anti-Christ, and the fake Jews that are white.

The Scripture tells us that Satan deceives the whole world,

> "*7 And there was war in heaven: Michael and his angels fought against the dragon; and the dragon fought and his angels,*
>
> *8 And prevailed not; neither was their place found any more in heaven.*
>
> *9 And the great dragon was cast out, that old serpent, called the Devil, and Satan, which deceiveth the whole world: he was cast out into the earth, and his angels were cast out with him."*
>
> *Revelation 12:7-9*

Satan is a deceiver. Tell us something we don't know. Tell us why it matters? Well, those that are deceived end up following Satan, thinking they are following God. Jesus even spoke about it,

> "*1 These things have I spoken unto you, that ye should not be offended.*
>
> *2 They shall put you out of the synagogues: yea, the time cometh, that whosoever killeth you will think that he doeth God service.*
>
> *3 And these things will they do unto you, because they have not known the Father, nor me."*
>
> *John 16:1-3*

Who You 'wit? The Case Against Fake White Jesus

This is the reason it matters who you follow. Paul warned of "another Jesus." This other "Jesus" is sent to lead you away from the one and only true Savior of the Israelites and those Gentiles that cleave to Israel. But how do you know the difference between the real Jesus or Yahshua ha'Maschiach as He is known in Hebrew and the fake white Jesus we have been taught to believe in by Constantine Christians, aka Western European Style Christianity? Yahshua, whom most ignorantly call Jesus, said we would know them by their fruit. So let's take a moment to look at the fruit:

If we use Scripture and not the traditions of men, we can clearly see that the "Jesus" that the European church fathers have given us is not the "Jesus" or Yahshua spoken of in Scripture. And this is why it matters. Yahshua ha'Maschiach has said,

> "²⁴ God is a Spirit: and they that worship Him must worship Him in spirit and in TRUTH."

> *John 4:24*

No matter what goes down, you will not make it through the Pearly Gates on a lie. We are in a time when knowledge has increased, so you MUST choose between Yahshua ha'Maschiach and fake white Jesus.

Let's take an even closer look at "Jesus Christ," the one Paul called "another Jesus." When Constantine stepped on the scene and convened the Council of Nicaea, he instituted changes that immediately led the newly minted Constantinian Roman Catholic Church astray. Those changes included moving the Sabbath worship from the last day of the week to the first day of the week. As many of the early believers had the habit of meeting on the first day of the week,

> "*7 And upon the first day of the week, when the disciples came together to break bread, Paul preached unto them, ready to depart on the morrow; and continued his speech until midnight.*"

> *Acts 20:7*

But a habit does not beget a Command. You can search the Scripture from front to back, and you will not find a single sentence from Abba Yah saying the Sabbath was to be done away with. In fact, as we have stated before,

> "*19 And He said unto us: 'Behold, I will separate unto Myself a people from among all the peoples, and these shall keep the Sabbath day, and I will sanctify them unto Myself as My people, and will bless them; as I have sanctified the Sabbath day and do sanctify (it) unto Myself, even so will I bless them, and they shall be My people and I will be their God.*
>
> *20 And I have chosen the seed of Jacob from amongst all that I have seen, and have written him down as My first-born son, and*

89

have sanctified him unto Myself for ever and ever; and I will teach them the Sabbath day, that they may keep Sabbath thereon from all work.'

²¹ And thus He created therein a sign in accordance with which they should keep Sabbath with us on the seventh day, to eat and to drink, and to bless Him who has created all things as He has blessed and sanctified unto Himself a peculiar people above all peoples, and that they should keep Sabbath together with us...

²⁸ And every one who observes it and keeps Sabbath thereon from all his work, will be holy and blessed throughout all days like unto us...

³⁰ And they shall not bring in nor take out from house to house on that day; for that day is more holy and blessed than any jubilee day of the jubilees; on this We kept Sabbath in the heavens before it was made known to any flesh to keep Sabbath thereon on the earth.

³¹ And the Creator of all things blessed it, but He did not sanctify all peoples and nations to keep Sabbath thereon, but Israel alone: them alone He permitted to eat and drink and to keep Sabbath thereon on the earth."

Jubilees 2:19-21, 28, 30-31

Our Elohim Yahuah T'Sebaoth, aka Abba Yah, The Ancient of Days, The Most High (TMH), our Heavenly Father chose Israel ALONE to keep the Sabbath. So don't get it twisted Negro, aka Black man, Israel, we are the beloved of TMH Abba Yah. We are the apple of His eye. And because we have gone away from Him, He has allowed us to go through the abuse that has been heaped upon us. And when His Son cracks the skies, He is only coming for those of His people that have followed Yahshua ha'Maschiach of Scripture, and He will destroy fake white Jesus, which is the IMAGE OF THE BEAST spoken of in Scripture and all those that follow the beast and his system.

Mixing the Holy with the Profane

Others have said that Constantine changed the worship day to Sunday because of the Roman tradition of sun worship. Whatever the reason, the Sabbath, which was established in heaven by Abba Yah, was cast aside in favor of Roman Sunday worship by the Gentiles and not TMH.

91

Then there is the matter of Christmas and Easter. The Gentiles were not given the Laws, Feast Days, or Covenant to keep as those were reserved for Israel ALONE. The Feast Days are a time of special remembrance and celebration of the goodness of Abba Yah.

Nowhere in Scripture do we find Abba Yah coming down the chimney on a silent night dropping off gifts for the children (or "cherrin" as my Grandmama used to say). However, in Western European Style Christianity, we find just that. Santa Claus, aka the fat cat in the red suit, knows whether you have been naughty or nice. ONLY the Elohim of all the universe knows this. The dude arrives in a sleigh led by a flying reindeer, with the lead reindeer having a glowing red nose. He comes down your chimney (where is the chimney in a rat-infested New York City apartment?) and leaves gifts underneath the Christmas tree.

People deck their homes with these trees that the Bible expressly tells you not to do,

> *"1 Hear ye the word which the LORD speaketh unto you, O house of Israel:*
>
> *2 Thus saith the LORD, Learn not the way of the heathen, and be not dismayed at the signs of heaven; for the heathen are dismayed at them.*

³ For the customs of the people are vain: for one cutteth a tree out of the forest, the work of the hands of the workman, with the axe.

⁴ They deck it with silver and with gold; they fasten it with nails and with hammers, that it move not.

⁵ They are upright as the palm tree, but speak not: they must needs be borne, because they cannot go. Be not afraid of them; for they cannot do evil, neither also is it in them to do good.

⁶ Forasmuch as there is none like unto Thee, O LORD; thou art great, and Thy name is great in might.

⁷ Who would not fear Thee, O King of nations? for to Thee doth it appertain: forasmuch as among all the wise men of the nations, and in all their kingdoms, there is none like unto Thee.

⁸ But they are altogether brutish and foolish: the stock is a doctrine of vanities.

⁹ Silver spread into plates is brought from Tarshish, and gold from Uphaz, the work of the workman, and of the hands of the founder: blue and purple is their clothing: they are all the work of cunning men. 10But the LORD is the true God, He is the living God, and an everlasting King: at His wrath the earth shall tremble, and the nations shall not be able to abide His indignation."

Jeremiah 10:1-10

Christmas trees are part of the worship package of the heathen that we were told specifically to avoid. Some say Christmas is the day Christians choose to celebrate the birth of Christ. Where in Scripture is this practice ordained by The Most High? This holiday came from Constantine with roots in the pagan celebration of the winter solstice. Also, December 25th according to pagan tradition, is the birth of Tammuz. Supposedly, Constantine took this heathen celebration, which was very popular among the Romans, and then renamed and rebranded it as the chief celebration of the newly instituted Christian faith known as the Roman Catholic Church, aka Western European Style Christianity, "the way of the heathen."

Mixing the Holy with the profane is an abomination in the eyes of The Most High,

> "*26* Her priests have violated My law, and have profaned Mine Holy things: they have put no difference between the Holy and profane, neither have they shewed difference between the unclean and the clean...
>
> *30* And I sought for a man among them, that should make up the hedge, and stand in the gap before Me for the land, that I should not destroy it: but I found none.
>
> *31* Therefore have I poured out Mine indignation upon them; I have consumed them with the fire of My wrath: their own way have I recompensed upon their heads, saith the Lord GOD."
>
> *Ezekiel 22:26, 30-31*

But the abomination didn't stop there. The heathen went even further with Easter or Ishtar worship,

> "*13* He said also unto me, Turn thee yet again, and thou shalt see greater abominations that they do.
>
> *14* Then He brought me to the door of the gate of the LORD'S house which was toward the north; and, behold, there sat women weeping for Tammuz.
>
> *15* Then said He unto me, Hast thou seen this, O son of man? turn thee yet again, and thou shalt see greater abominations than these.

16 And He brought me into the inner court of the LORD'S house, and, behold, at the door of the temple of the LORD, between the porch and the altar, were about five and twenty men, with their backs toward the temple of the LORD, and their faces toward the east; and they worshipped the sun toward the east.

17 Then He said unto me, Hast thou seen this, O son of man? Is it a light thing to the House of Judah that they commit the abominations which they commit here? for they have filled the land with violence, and have returned to provoke Me to anger: and, lo, they put the branch to their nose.

18 Therefore will I also deal in fury: Mine eye shall not spare, neither will I have pity: and though they cry in Mine ears with a loud voice, yet will I not hear them."

Ezekiel 8:13-18

What? Weeping for Tammuz? What is He talking about? Ishtar, which is pronounced "EASTER," is the worship of the fertility goddess. This fertility goddess is none other than Semiramis, Nimrod's mother who conceived a son named Tammuz with her son Nimrod. This leads us to the question, "is your daddy your brother?" This abominable incestuous relationship is the basis of Easter or Ishtar. Yet no Roman Catholic, aka Western European Style Christian Church talks about why they celebrate Easter over Passover.

95

And, of course, any self-respecting member of the Western European Style Christian Church will vehemently deny any association with the Catholic Church. But when you study their traditions, there is no difference in the belief system. Both belief in a fake white Jesus. They both believe in Christmas and Easter. They both believe that the true Israelite people are these Western European imposters in the Land today, as pointed out earlier.

The only difference between Catholicism and Protestantism is Martin Luther's 95 Thesis. When you read the 95 Thesis, his only beef with Rome was the selling of indulgences. He had no beef with Rome over the enslavement of Black folks, aka Hebrews, that had not received Western European Style Christianity. If anything, he encouraged it as it was reported that he hated the Yahudeen with a passion. Outside of the selling of indulgences, he was one with the Church at Rome. As has been reported in this book, the Roman Catholic Church was behind the legalization of the Trans-Atlantic Slave Trade, which was owned and operated almost exclusively by the fake jakes. Is there anything that Europeans do that isn't fake outside of a propensity to steal, kill, and destroy? But I digress.

Christmas, Easter, and almost total agreement with Rome means you have to pick a side. Western European Style Christianity or your Hebraic culture, which is the Bible. So who are you going to follow, Black man?

We have pointed out how what is called Christianity of today is nothing more than warmed-over Catholicism, which is none other than Baal worship meant to deceive the children of Israel

97

into once again bowing down before Satan as opposed to bowing before the ONLY true God, our Elohim Yahuah, aka Yah, aka The Most High, Abba Yah, the Father.

The Christian Church is the Church of Satan?

Finally, in the Book of Mormon, which is another book stolen from our culture and rebranded as part of another European offshoot of Christianity, we find this,

> *"8 And it came to pass that when the angel had spoken these words, he said unto me: Rememberest thou the Covenants of the Father unto the House of Israel? I said unto him, Yea.*
>
> *9 And it came to pass that he said unto me: Look, and behold that great and abominable church, which is the mother of abominations, whose founder is the devil.*
>
> *10 And he said unto me: Behold there are save TWO CHURCHES ONLY; one is the Church of the Lamb of God, and the other is the church of the devil; wherefore, whoso belongeth not to the Church of the Lamb of God belongeth to that great church, which is the mother of abominations; and she is the whore of all the earth.*
>
> *11 And it came to pass that I looked and beheld the whore of all the earth, and she sat upon many waters; and she had dominion over all the earth, among all nations, kindreds, tongues, and people.*
>
> *12 And it came to pass that I beheld the Church of the Lamb of God, and its numbers were few, because of the wickedness and abominations of the whore who sat upon many waters; nevertheless, I beheld that the Church of the Lamb, who were the saints of God, were also upon all the face of the earth; and*

their dominions upon the face of the earth were small, because of the wickedness of the great whore whom I saw.

[13] And it came to pass that I beheld that the great mother of abominations did gather together multitudes upon the face of all the earth, among all the nations of the Gentiles, to fight against the Lamb of God.

[14] And it came to pass that I, Nephi, beheld the power of the Lamb of God, that it descended upon the saints of the Church of the Lamb, and upon the Covenant people of the Lord, who were scattered upon all the face of the earth; and they were armed with righteousness and with the power of God in great glory.

[15] And it came to pass that I beheld that the wrath of God was poured out upon that great and abominable church, insomuch that there were wars and rumors of wars among all the nations and kindreds of the earth.

[16] And as there began to be wars and rumors of wars among all the nations which belonged to the mother of abominations, the angel spake unto me, saying: Behold, the wrath of God is upon the mother of harlots; and behold, thou seest all these things—

[17] And when the day cometh that the wrath of God is poured out upon the mother of harlots, which is the great and abominable church of all the earth, whose founder is the devil, then, at that day, the work of the Father shall commence, in preparing the way for the fulfilling of His Covenants, which He hath made to His people who are of the House of Israel."

1 Nephi 14:8-17

The book of Revelation puts it this way,

"[1] And there came one of the seven angels which had the seven vials, and talked with me, saying unto me, Come hither; I will shew unto thee the judgment of the great whore that sitteth upon many waters:

[2] With whom the kings of the earth have committed fornication, and the inhabitants of the earth have been made drunk with the wine of her fornication.

99

3 So he carried me away in the spirit into the wilderness: and I saw a woman sit upon a scarlet coloured beast, full of names of blasphemy, having seven heads and ten horns.

4 And the woman was arrayed in purple and scarlet colour, and decked with gold and precious stones and pearls, having a golden cup in her hand full of abominations and filthiness of her fornication:

5 And upon her forehead was a name written, MYSTERY, BABYLON THE GREAT, THE MOTHER OF HARLOTS AND ABOMINATIONS OF THE EARTH.

6 And I saw the woman drunken with the blood of the saints, and with the blood of the martyrs of Jesus: and when I saw her, I wondered with great admiration.

7 And the angel said unto me, Wherefore didst thou marvel? I will tell thee the mystery of the woman, and of the beast that carrieth her, which hath the seven heads and ten horns.

8 The beast that thou sawest was, and is not; and shall ascend out of the bottomless pit, and go into perdition: and they that dwell on the earth shall wonder, whose names were not written in the book of life from the foundation of the world, when they behold the beast that was, and is not, and yet is.

9 And here is the mind which hath wisdom. The seven heads are seven mountains, on which the woman sitteth...

13 These have one mind, and shall give their power and strength unto the beast.

14 These shall make war with the Lamb, and the Lamb shall overcome them: for he is Lord of lords, and King of kings: and they that are with him are called, and chosen, and faithful.

15 And he saith unto me, The waters which thou sawest, where the whore sitteth, are peoples, and multitudes, and nations, and tongues. 16 And the ten horns which thou sawest upon the beast, these shall hate the whore, and shall make her desolate and naked, and shall eat her flesh, and burn her with fire.

[17] For God hath put in their hearts to fulfil his will, and to agree, and give their kingdom unto the beast, until the words of God shall be fulfilled.

[18] And the woman which thou sawest is that great city, which reigneth over the kings of the earth."

Revelation 17:1-9, 13-17

So now we know there are only two churches, the Church of the Lamb of Yah and the church of the devil. Because there are only two churches, there are only two choices. This means that it does matter who you align yourself with. The Scripture is clear everywhere you look that in the end, most will join forces together with the devil and his seed to fight against the Lamb of Yah, the Son of TMH Yah, Yahshua ha'Maschiach and His Chosen people, the so-called Negroes, and those strangers and Gentiles that have been chosen by Abba Yah.

Know Them by Their Fruit

Now we have to determine who these people are. Yahshua ha'Maschiach, whom most ignorantly call Jesus, said,

"[15] Beware of false prophets, which come to you in sheep's clothing, but inwardly they are ravening wolves.

[16] Ye shall know them by their fruits. Do men gather grapes of thorns, or figs of thistles?

[17] Even so every good tree bringeth forth good fruit; but a corrupt tree bringeth forth evil fruit.

101

¹⁸ A good tree cannot bring forth evil fruit, neither can a corrupt tree bring forth good fruit.

¹⁹ Every tree that bringeth not forth good fruit is hewn down, and cast into the fire.

²⁰ Wherefore by their fruits ye shall know them."

Matthew 7:15-20

What is the fruit of those that follow after Satan?

"¹⁰ The thief cometh not, but for to steal, and to kill, and to destroy: I am come that they might have life, and that they might have it more abundantly."

John 10:10

When we look at the fruit of the Gentiles, what do we find? Theft, death, and destruction EVERYWHERE they are found. Old World Europeans aside, let's look just at what they have done in the New World. Beginning with the Renaissance Period and Dum Diversas, we find that this alignment with Satan is the overarching theme of European rule.

Deal with the Devil

Dum Diversas and the other Papal Bulls that followed authorized the most heinous forms of slavery ever known to mankind. As was pointed out previously, these proclamations condemned the enslaved to perpetual slavery that they could never be freed from. Millions upon millions of Negroes, aka

Hebrews, were sent throughout the Americas as slaves, and millions more died being transported through the proceeding years. The blatant disregard for Hebrew life was on a scale that was and is unimaginable. Yet this was already foretold in the Scripture that because of our disobedience,

> *"⁴⁹ The LORD shall bring a nation against thee from far, from the end of the earth, as swift as the eagle flieth; a nation whose tongue thou shalt not understand;*
>
> *⁵⁰ A nation of fierce countenance, which shall not regard the person of the old, nor shew favour to the young:"*

> *Deuteronomy 28:49-50*

So, they kicked off their agreement with Satan with a bang. It has been said that Europeans, aka Gentiles, Caucasians, have NEVER lived peaceably with any other people anywhere at any time. And they have always worshipped pagan gods and pagan deities. They swept through the Middle East (which until the Suez Canal was known as NE Africa, after all the animals and vegetation, are truly African) and down into Egypt, which is a scant 200 miles away, and as is their custom, they supplant the people that are in the area and try to become them. Lest we forget, Ptolemy sat on the throne as Pharaoh. It's what the sons of Japheth in conjunction with Esau did,

> *"¹² And to the angel of the church in Pergamos write; These things saith he which hath the sharp sword with two edges;*
>
> *¹³ I know thy works, and where thou dwellest, even where Satan's seat is: and thou holdest fast My name, and hast not*

103

denied My faith, even in those days wherein Antipas was My faithful martyr, who was slain among you, where Satan dwelleth.

[14] But I have a few things against thee, because thou hast there them that hold the doctrine of Balaam, who taught Balak to cast a stumbling block before the children of Israel, to eat things sacrificed unto idols, and to commit fornication."

Revelation 2:12-14

And so we find that the seat of Satan is firmly ensconced within the dwelling place of these same European or Gentile people that swallowed up much of Esau's seed and have gone throughout all of the earth causing death and destruction everywhere they go. These are Satan's people that Yahshua is talking about. The proof is in the pudding. Let's eat.

They Steal

"[48] And laid open the book of the law, wherein the heathen had sought to paint the likeness of their images."

1 Maccabees 3:48

If Europeans do nothing else, they steal. One of their favorite things to do after conquering other people is to "honor" them by stealing their identity. Everywhere Japheth and Esau go, the first thing they do is steal the land from the people that are already there. Once they steal the land of the indigenous people, they assume their identity. When Alexander the Greek swept into the

Middle East and Asia Minor, they defeated a completely black population as all of Mesopotamia was Nimrod's Kingdom. He, of course, was a descendant of Ham. Once Alexander conquered the land, his Macedonian people moved into those areas and supplanted the people that were there, took over their identity, and claim to be them. That is why you see the land of Ham now populated by Europeans claiming to be the original black Arabs that inhabited the land from antiquity. And it is why many Europeans believe that the Egyptians were Caucasian people when there is not ONE image of a white-skinned Egyptian painted on the walls of the Egyptian tombs.

That was just the warm-up act. When they moved into Europe, there were already black Hebrews ruling in the British Isles. In fact, many have said that King James was actually a

Hebrew Israelite and therefore a Black man. When looking at a portrait of his father, who clearly was a Black man, you must question what you've been told.

We know now that the Hebrews, who were and are a Black people, ruled in the British Isles for approximately 800 years. But once again, our European enemies removed the original black people's images and replaced them with images of themselves. And then claimed that they have always been white people.

In fact, the name Europe itself was taken from a black princess named Europa.

They just dropped the black image and description of her and kept it moving. After a few decades, no one brought it up, and no one remembered. Now when you think of Europe, you have no knowledge of who she was, and that originally Europe was ruled by Black people, aka Hebrews, which is where all the Hebraic names came from. Once again, they moved into an area and assumed the identity of the people that were already there.

You Lookin' for Me?

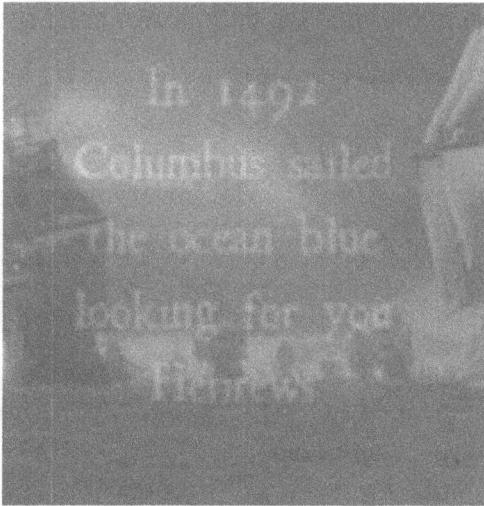

And as soon as they landed, the first thing they did was set their sites on stealing the land from the people that were already there. Columbus reported back to his benefactors that the people were virtually unarmed, and with a small army, they could take possession of all that they saw and claim it for the Crown. The theft was so easy that the rest of Europe joined the fray and the only real fight was between the European nations competing to get the biggest and best slice of the pie.

Columbus reports that the people were black with woolly hair. Their portraits all show indigenous people that looked like Africans, just as he'd been told. In fact, ALL of the people they had encountered were black people. Later they tried to cover the fact that the people were black by saying they were cooper colored people. As if there is a dime's worth of difference between cooper color and the dark brown color of the Africans they had encountered elsewhere in the world. Next time you have a penny, put it next to your skin.

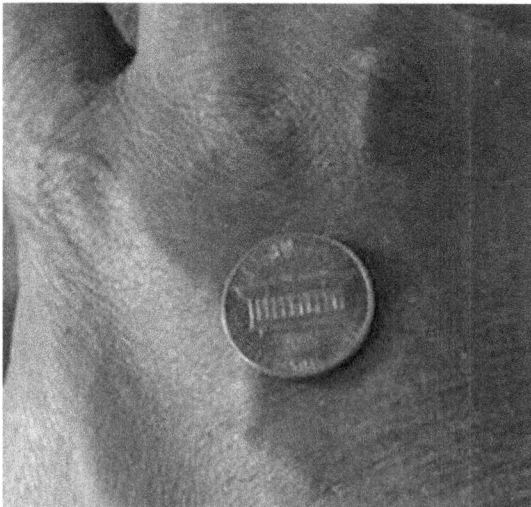

But being who they are, they fed us the same drivel line as they did with fake white Jesus. They read the Scripture but gave us an image of something else and began calling the indigenous people the slaves that were brought over from African, and the imported Europeans that mixed with the natives were now called the indigenous people. Once again, they literally stole the indigenous people's identity from them while they were standing there in the room.

'If you tell a lie long enough, strong enough, and with a big enough gun pointed at their cranium to make sure they understand that its agreement or death, then the people will believe.'

Theft is their Jam

Noah divided the lands of the earth between his sons as was pointed out in Scripture,

> "29 This is the land which came forth for Japheth and his sons as the portion of his inheritance which he should possess for himself and his sons, for their generations for ever; five great islands, and a great land in the north.
>
> 30 But it is cold, and the land of Ham is hot, and the land of Shem is neither hot nor cold, but it is of blended cold and heat."
>
> Jubilees 8:29-30

The Europeans not only steal lands, but they also steal cultures and inventions. In fact, for the most part, they steal everything in sight. What about the case of Jack Daniels Whiskey? Here is one of the world's top alcoholic brands worth billions of dollars. It has made the founders fabulously wealthy. Yet now we find out the man behind the brand that gave them the recipe was a Black man named Nathan "Nearest" Green. They would not have even mentioned his name were it not for a black author, Fawn Weaver, who picked up the story while on vacation in SINGAPORE. That's right, this sister heard about this story by chance on vacation ten thousand miles from home. Once caught, they offered up a mention of Nearest Green. No stock, no ownership. Just a paragraph.

What about a series of Black comedies during the 70s? Good Times, The Jefferson's, What's Happening, and the movie Cooley High. Eric Monte was the creator of all of these classic Black comedies. But his two biggest hits do not have his name on them. Instead, we find that the "Official" creator was Norman Lear. It turns out that Mr. Monte had to sue Lear and others for stealing his ideas and not paying him his fair share. Having been surrounded on all sides by Lear's allies, including his agent and lawyer, Monte settled for one million dollars. Included in the settlement was giving creator credit to Norman Lear for both shows. Monte was subsequently blackballed in Hollywood and ended up in a shelter in Southern California while Lear built one of the biggest Hollywood fortunes ever, mainly on the strength

110

of the residuals from reruns of shows created by a Black man. These shows continue to produce millions yearly in syndication fees. Theft is what they do. And they do it in broad daylight out in the open with no shame.

They kill

Murder is the case that we gave them—187 on the mutha fuggin' block. We rap about it and do it to each other just like we've been trained to do. Esau-Edom, with their Neanderthal fallen angel DNA, aka the seed of Satan, go out and do it to the world.

"11 If they say, Come with us, let us lay wait for blood, let us lurk privily for the innocent without cause:

12 Let us swallow them up alive as the grave; and whole, as those that go down into the pit:

13 We shall find all precious substance, we shall fill our houses with spoil:"

Proverbs 1:11-13

If you know nothing else about the children of Japheth and Esau, know and understand that they are ruthless killers in

111

pursuit of the bag. No one commits mass murder with more efficiency and aplomb than these people. When they descended upon our forefathers in 70AD at Jerusalem, they killed everything and everyone in sight. No one and nothing was spared.

The Romans and Europeans, in general, invented new and ruthless ways of killing people. Simple death was not good enough for these people. When the Romans killed people, they made sure the torture was especially brutal. During biblical times, crucifixion was a favorite slow and painful way to kill.

With the voyage to the New World, the killing machine has gone into overdrive,

> *"5 If thieves came to thee, if robbers by night, (how art thou cut off!) would they not have stolen till they had enough? if the grape gatherers came to thee, would they not leave some grapes?"*

Obadiah 1:5

When Columbus and His men descended upon the natives of the islands, they immediately claimed the area for the Crown, took captives, and began their killing spree. Columbus noted that the people were virtually unarmed, and with a small force, they could take the area with minimal effort. He returned to Spain with samples of what was available in this new land. He gained the backing of the Royal Crown to go back with a bigger force, and from there, they set up shops among these Negro people, and within less than a generation, they killed ninety percentage or over seventy million of the indigenous people who were what Columbus believed were the Lost Tribes of Israel.

American Philosophy
From Wounded Knee to the Present

Indigenous people north and south were displaced, died of disease, and were killed by Europeans through slavery, rape, and war. In 1491, about 145 million people lived in the western hemisphere. By 1691, the population of indigenous Americans had **DECLINED BY 90-95 PERCENT,** or by around 130 million people.
pg 375

Once again, they did their favorite magic trick which was to kill nearly all of the inhabitants and then assume their identity. Most of Latin America is considered to be white or European. In fact, they are the descendants of the Spanish conquistadors and other Europeans who came to the New World and raped the women of the country to "lighten" the color of the people. Much of South and Central America turned to this Blanqueamiento strategy as their national strategy. They sent in white men with the express purpose of intermingling their heathen seed with the indigenous Negro people. They didn't just kill people; they killed everything. They went through North America and killed off a seemingly inexhaustible supply of buffalo for sport. The natives that were here lived in harmony with the animals and the environment that was here. However, these European people have a scorched earth mentality. They cannot help themselves. It is their nature to kill.

> *"16 These six things doth the LORD hate: yea, seven are an abomination unto Him:*
>
> *17 A proud look, a lying tongue, and hands that shed innocent blood,*
>
> *18 An heart that deviseth wicked imaginations, feet that be swift in running to mischief,*
>
> *19 A false witness that speaketh lies, and he that soweth discord among brethren."*
>
> Proverbs 6:16-19

Now, back to the murder at hand. Consider that in WW1 and WWll, Europeans killed over one hundred million of their own people. However, they have no problem portraying every other people as savages and murderers. In the Trans Atlantic Slave Trade, they estimated that another fifty to sixty million died in the Middle Passage. As stated earlier, ninety percent of the natives living in the New World were exterminated, which they themselves estimated to be upwards of seventy to one hundred million people.

They destroy

Malak Yesha'Yahu ben Yahudah

"²⁴ The earth is given into the hand of the wicked: he covereth the faces of the judges thereof; if not, where, and who is he?"

Job 9:24

The wicked are the people from the north. The sons of Japheth that mixed with Esau and the Neanderthals, which many say are the Nephilim or fallen angels,

"¹ And after some days my son Methuselah took a wife for his son Lamech, and she became pregnant by him and bore a son.

² And HIS BODY WAS WHITE as snow and red as the blooming of a rose, and the hair of his head and his long locks were white as wool, and his eyes beautiful. And when he opened his eyes, he lighted up the whole house like the sun, and the whole house was very bright.

³ And thereupon he arose in the hands of the midwife, opened his mouth, and conversed with the Lord of righteousness.

⁴ And his father Lamech was afraid of him and fled, and came to his father Methuselah.

⁵ And he said unto him: 'I have begotten a strange son, diverse from and unlike man, and RESEMBLING THE SONS OF THE GOD OF HEAVEN; and his nature is different and he is not like us, and his eyes are as the rays of the sun, and his countenance is glorious.

⁶ And it seems to me that he is not sprung from me but from the angels, and I fear that in his days a wonder may be wrought on the earth."

Enoch 106:1-6

So the angels of God must have white skin as Lamech says his son has white skin unlike mankind and looks like the sons of God who were the angels and, in this case, the fallen angels. Noah then was the first albino. But more importantly, white skin

115

is synonymous with the fallen angels. Those same fallen angels came down and produced offspring with the black women that were here

Neanderthal French for Nephilim or Fallen Angels?

Scientists have found a different species of mankind outside of the human gene pool called Neanderthal, which is only found in the northern regions of the globe. These Neanderthal had white skin and straight hair. These same scientists confirm that the white skin and straight hair come from Neanderthal genes. They also confirm that the only 100% pure humans are Africans that have not mixed with Europeans, Asians, and East Indians.

Until the birth of Noah, no one had ever been described as having white skin. Therefore, outside of albinism, scientists have discovered the only other contribution to white skin is Neanderthal admixture. One of the characteristics of the fallen angels is their propensity towards destruction. They destroyed everything in their wake, including the man whom Abba Yah has created,

> *"¹ And all the others (fallen angels) together with them took unto themselves wives, and each chose for himself one, and they began to go in unto them and to defile themselves with them, and they taught them charms and enchantments, and the cutting of roots, and made them acquainted with plants.*
>
> *² And they became pregnant, and they bare great giants, whose height was three thousand ells:*
>
> *³ Who consumed all the acquisitions of men. And when men could no longer sustain them,*
>
> *⁴ the giants turned against them and devoured mankind.*
>
> *⁵ And they began to sin against birds, and beasts, and reptiles, and fish, and to devour one another's flesh, and drink the blood.*
>
> *⁶ Then the earth laid accusation against the lawless ones."*
>
> *Book of Enoch 7:1-6*

Now, back to the lecture at hand. All the white-skinned nations have one thing in common, and that is the destruction of everything around them. They do not live in harmony with anyone or anything at any time or anywhere, just like the fallen angels.

Because we sinned against our God, He said He would bring the nations from the north to wreak havoc upon Israel. Destruction is part of their genetic makeup. They cannot help themselves; it is how they are programmed. And they have been on assignment from Abba Yah since the time of Yahshua ha'Maschiach to track down and destroy His people,

> "*⁵ Declare ye in Judah, and publish in Jerusalem; and say, Blow ye the trumpet in the land: cry, gather together, and say, Assemble yourselves, and let us go into the defenced cities.*
>
> *⁶ Set up the standard toward Zion: retire, stay not: for I will bring evil from the north, and a great destruction.*
>
> *⁷ The lion is come up from his thicket, and the destroyer of the Gentiles is on His way; He is gone forth from His place to make thy land desolate; and thy cities shall be laid waste, without an inhabitant."*
>
> *Jeremiah 4:5-7*

The Scripture tells us that Isaac prophesied that Esau would receive everything he has by the sword or violence,

> "*³⁸ And Esau said unto his father, Hast thou but one blessing, my father? bless me, even me also, O my father. And Esau lifted up his voice, and wept.*
>
> *³⁹ And Isaac his father answered and said unto him, Behold, thy dwelling shall be the fatness of the earth, and of the dew of heaven from above;*
>
> *⁴⁰ And by thy sword shalt thou live, and shalt serve thy brother; and it shall come to pass when thou shalt have the dominion, that thou shalt break his yoke from off thy neck."*
>
> *Genesis 27:38-40*

They came down out of the Caucasus mountains and attacked everything in sight. And they made their way to Mt. Seir, where the descendants of Esau lived. A Great War ensued between Kittim, aka Chittim, Romim, Romans. The children of

Esau were defeated and absorbed into Kittim, aka Chittim's empire,

> *"2 And Abianus king of Chittim went forth in that year, that is in the thirty-first year of his reign, and a great force with him of the mighty men of the children of Chittim, and he went to Seir to fight against the children of Esau.*
>
> *3 And Hadad the king of Edom heard of his report, and he went forth to meet him with a heavy people and strong force and engaged in battle with him in the field of Edom.*
>
> *4 And the hand of Chittim prevailed over the children of Esau, and the children of Chittim slew of the children of Esau, two and twenty thousand men, and all the children of Esau fled from before them.*
>
> *5 And the children of Chittim pursued them and they reached Hadad king of Edom, who was running before them and they caught him alive, and brought him to Abianus king of Chittim.*
>
> *6 And Abianus ordered him to be slain, and Hadad king of Edom died in the forty-eighth year of his reign.*
>
> *7 And the children of Chittim continued their pursuit of Edom, and they smote them with a great slaughter and Edom became subject to the children of Chittim.*
>
> *8 And the children of Chittim ruled over Edom, and Edom became under the hand of the children of Chittim and became one kingdom from that day.*
>
> *9 And from that time they could no more lift up their heads, and their kingdom became one with the children of Chittim.*
>
> *10 And Abianus placed officers in Edom and all the children of Edom became subject and tributary to Abianus, and Abianus turned back to his own land, Chittim.*
>
> *11 And when he returned he renewed his government and built for himself a spacious and fortified palace for a royal residence, and reigned securely over the children of Chittim and over Edom."*

And for those that don't get the connection between the Romans and Chittim, the book of Jasher helps you get the understanding you seek,

> *"¹⁶And the children of Chittim are the Romim who dwell in the valley of Canopia by the river Tibreu."*

Jasher 10:16

And so you have the recipe for the most destructive gene pool ever designed. And they do not disappoint. There has never been a pollution problem anywhere globally except where people with Neanderthal, Japheth, and Esau genetics are found.

The lust for gain overshadows any sense of obligation to protect the environment or future generations against the all-out quest for maximum profit right now almost exactly like the fallen angels' offspring spoken of in the Book of Enoch. The future be damned they gotta get paid today. That's their fruit.

By the early 1960s, most major US cities were cesspools of toxic rivers, polluted skies, and industrial waste. Lake Erie was so polluted that the lake's water caught on fire at least ten times, with 1969 being the most notable. How does the water catch on fire? Smog in Los Angeles was so thick that flying into LA you could see the brown haze from at least 50 miles away. NYC had virtually the same problem.

But that's child's play compared to the other destruction that they have caused elsewhere. When the Europeans in North America destroyed the beautiful pristine landscape that was here, they went into the plains and where there were once buffalo and bison for as far as the eye could see, they destroyed the food supply that fed and clothed the Natives for millennia within a few short years. The Natives remarked that they killed for sport instead of need.

Then there is the coral reef in the tropical areas of the world like the Barrier Reef. These reefs have been around since the dawn of time; now, after the wicked have been in charge, reefs worldwide have become graveyards. Once teeming with life, much of the 1,400mile-long reef is dead. As usual, Europeans blame the cause on some nameless, faceless entity rather than on the true culprit... white-skinned nations that control the planet.

As the Scripture says,

"2 When the righteous are in authority, the people rejoice: but when the wicked beareth rule, the people mourn."

Proverbs 29:2

When the Europeans showed up in the Middle East, the people mourned. When they showed up in Africa, the people wept. When they showed up in the Americas, the people

122

mourned. When they showed up in Australia, the people grieved. When they showed up in Asia, the people lamented. How is it that this one people goes into every land throughout the world that was previously peaceful and prosperous and then destroys the people, the environment, and the way of life within a few years? They do this everywhere they go?

These are the people that fit the description of those that STEAL, KILL, and DESTROY as the Scripture has said. And these are the people that are the enemy of the one true and living God, Yahuah. And these are the people that Yahshua ha'Maschiach is coming back to destroy.

His People, his people

As mentioned earlier, Abba Yah has shown me that He has a Christ and a people that look like Him. And Satan has an anti-Christ and a people that look like him.

Abba Yah's Christ came through the Hebrew, Israelites who were and are the so-called Negroes. A people that were friendly, sharing, and caring to a fault. Who else allows people into their community that they know hate them, prey upon them, while stealing and killing their men, women, and children at will.

These same people then turn around and say, "Lord, forgive them for they know not what they do."

Malcolm said it best, "As long as they've been doing what they're doing, they are experts at it. They know exactly what they're doing." When Dillon Roof went to church and prayed with those Black folks, then, he got up off his knees and killed everybody in sight. Abba Yah blessed our foolish and naive hearts. Our people were all in line forgiving this dastardly deed before the bodies hit the floor. And he was repaid by his brothers and friends in blue with a leisurely drive to the county lockup complete with a stop at Burger King as an "Attaboy" for a job well done.

When Botham "SHEM" Jean was gunned down like a dog by a police officer on duty while innocently sitting on his couch in his own home having a nice bowl of ice cream, his brother, his father, and the judge "Mammy Tammy" as she became known couldn't wait to stand in line to offer hugs with words of apology and forgiveness for the murder's plight. Not the plight of the brother that was slaughtered in his own home simply eating ice cream and enjoying a quiet Friday night at home alone. Mammy Tammy offered up not a year or work condolence for the young brother Joshua Brown that was suspiciously killed after his testimony (what idiot who was in fear of his life for

124

testifying against the officer would turn around and go out to buy drugs? It smells of a state-sponsored hit. Thanks to the right-winger, Alex Jones, we know they do these kinds of hits all the time).

And then, just this week, a young brother, Jacob Blake was gunned down by police in front of his children for the express crime of trying to be a peacemaker and break up a fight. And that was followed up by another white supremacist who showed up at the protests and gunned down two more people and escaped the scene of the crime by simply walking by police murder weapon in hand without them so much as asking why this white man would feel the need to show up at a black protest armed to the teeth only to be quietly arrested at home a few days later.

Police were seen on camera offering words of encouragement and thanks while handing bottled water to the shooter and other European militia moments before murdering unarmed protestors.

In the words of that old Negro spiritual,

"Hold (the "d" is silent where I come from) the F*CK up. These Mutha F##**%s (in my best Samuel L voice) just murdered our sons in cold blood and we apologizin' to them? Nah, hell to the nizzle baby, we ain't goin' out like that."

I'm sorry. Perhaps they didn't quite sing it that way where you come from. See, I'm even apologizing. It's what we do.

125

Now, if we could only convince our people to apologize to Abba Yah for trying to bless us above all nations the way we apologize to Massa for killing us without remorse, maybe He will find it in His heart to forgive us our sin and cleanse us from all unrighteousness.

You Twitchin' Baby, You Twitchin'

Then, there is Satan and his crowd.

When OJ was tried and found not guilty, did the Europeans say, "Forgive him, Lord, it was a crime of passion, and he just lost his head for a moment?" Absolutely not. Fred Goldman, the father of Ron, when asked if he forgave OJ, said, "HELL NO."

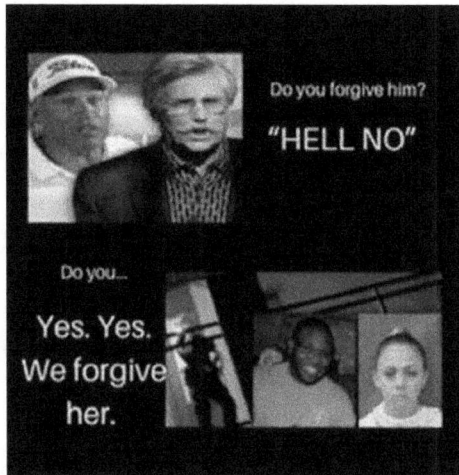

And the white community, including these so-called evangelical Christians, joined in unison to hunt down OJ for ten or fifteen years until they could finally nail him on the charge of attempted robbery for trying to retrieve the stuff that was stolen from him. The officer in charge of the investigation was quoted as saying, "We got him."

So there is a difference between His Chosen people and Satan's people. In these last days, with all the eyes trained on Esau-Edom with their Neanderthal blood cannot help themselves. They are starting to twitch. They are returning to their natural selves and character of rape, robbery, murder, and destruction in front of the whole world with everyone watching. They simply cannot stop themselves. It's who they are.

We Must Return to Our Heritage

So, it matters whether or not you know and understand who's who in these end times. As stated in the chart above, Yahshua kept the law, and those that follow Him must keep the Law too. After all, didn't He say to the rich young man that asked Him about eternal life,

"16 And, behold, one came and said unto Him, Good Master, what good thing shall I do, that I may have eternal life?

127

[17] And He said unto Him, Why callest thou Me good? there is none good but One, that is, God: but if thou wilt enter into life, KEEP THE COMMANDMENTS."

Matthew 19:16-17

We have shown that the Israelites spoken of in the Scripture are the so-called Negro because ONLY our experience matches the prophecies. Only Negroes have been enslaved all over the world. At the foundation of every society on earth today, there is a Negro slave. Negro slaves built the foundation of Western civilization. Negro slaves were the ones that worked the sugar cane plantations and the cotton plantations that made Europe fabulously wealthy. They won't tell you that France's wealth is extracted yearly off West African countries' backs. The French admit that without the wealth of Africa, they would be a third world country,

> *"Without Africa, France will slide down into the rank of a third [rate] power."*

President Jacques Chirac

England, to this day, gets much of its wealth from the resources extorted out of the West Indies. Right now, the wealth of Jamaica is exported to the queen every year. They won't tell you that Belgium still profits from the resources of the Congo. The wealth of every European nation is in some way tied to the theft of Negro, aka Israelite labor or land.

"⁴ They have said, Come, and let us cut them off from being a nation; that the name of Israel may be no more in remembrance.

⁵ For they have consulted together with one consent: they are confederate against thee:"

Psalms 83:4-5

Lest we forget, there are others of the heathen and our own people that have joined with the primary abusers and oppressors of true Israel. Like the people currently called Arabs. Even they have gotten in on the act. They operate open-air slave markets in Libya to this day. They lure young women into their countries as servants and enslave them once they are there. There are countless stories and even videos of both the men and the women beating, maiming, raping, and murdering these young, primarily Hebrew women. There is even a video of one young sister who somehow was put into the position of climbing out onto the ledge of a six or seven-story building and was holding on for dear life. She lost her grip and fell to her death. All the while, her Arab captors were screaming and taunting her. So the barbaric treatment extends far beyond the European people.

And don't think the treatment of Abba Yah's people by Asians has escaped His notice. They move their businesses into our communities and extract billions of dollars while mistreating and even beating and murdering our people. If you were in the US back in the 90s, everyone recalls the case of Latasha Harlins,

129

a young Black Hebrew girl that was shot in the back over a dispute about a bottle of orange juice. The Korean shop owner that worked in concert with the Jewish judge asked the judge to ensure that the Asian shop owner only got probation.

We see videos of Asian shop owners in our community physically abusing our sisters daily. And now, the abuse has gone international as the Chinese have begun moving into African countries with large Hebrew populations. They have learned well from their European partners. They come with smiles and assurances of help with no agenda. They offer loans that cannot be repaid to Hamitic leaders installed over our Hebrew people, who pocket much of the money and allow these Asian thieves to walk away with ownership of the country's greatest resources.

But our God has a response for these people. All of them,

"16 Therefore all they that devour thee (Israel aka Negroes) shall be devoured; and all thine adversaries, every one of them, shall go into captivity; and they that spoil thee shall be a spoil, and all that prey upon thee will I give for a prey."

Jeremiah 30:16

And for Asia, he specifically says,

"46 And thou, Asia, that art partaker of the hope of Babylon, and art the glory of her person:

47 Woe be unto thee, thou wretch, because thou hast made thyself like unto her; and hast decked thy daughters in whoredom, that they might please and glory in thy lovers, which have always desired to commit whoredom with thee.

[48] *Thou hast followed her that is hated in all her works and inventions: therefore saith God,*

[49] *I will send plagues upon thee; widowhood, poverty, famine, sword, and pestilence, to waste thy houses with destruction and death."*

2 Esdras 15:46-49

All of these people that abuse the so-called Negro, aka the Apple of God's Eye, will be destroyed. EVERY SINGLE ONE OF THEM. These are the seed of the serpent. These are the ones mixed with Neanderthal blood who have the nature of their father. They cannot help themselves. Within the seed of the Europeans is the seed of Esau. He has within him a hatred for the children of Israel that drives him,

"[1] Moreover the word of the LORD came unto me, saying,

[2] *Son of man, set thy face against mount Seir, and prophesy against it,*

[3] *And say unto it, Thus saith the Lord GOD; Behold, O mount Seir, I am against thee, and I will stretch out mine hand against thee, and I will make thee most desolate.*

[4] *I will lay thy cities waste, and thou shalt be desolate, and thou shalt know that I am the LORD.*

[5] *Because thou hast had a perpetual hatred, and hast shed the blood of the children of Israel by the force of the sword in the time of their calamity, in the time that their iniquity had an end:*

[6] *Therefore, as I live, saith the Lord GOD, I will prepare thee unto blood, and blood shall pursue thee: sith thou hast not hated blood, even blood shall pursue thee.*

131

7 Thus will I make mount Seir most desolate, and cut off from it him that passeth out and him that returneth.

8 And I will fill his mountains with his slain men: in thy hills, and in thy valleys, and in all thy rivers, shall they fall that are slain with the sword.

9 I will make thee perpetual desolations, and thy cities shall not return: and ye shall know that I am the LORD."

Ezekiel 35:1-9

We know that once TMH puts His mouth against you, there is no way of escape. The punishment must be carried out. And let us be clear, not all of Esau is mixed in with the Europeans. There is a significant portion that still lives in Africa among the Hebrews and the Hamites. They know who they are and live openly as the children of Esau. TMH spent an entire book of the Bible dedicated to the cursing and destruction of the children of Esau, aka Edom, Idumea,

"1 The vision of Obadiah. Thus saith the Lord GOD concerning Edom; We have heard a rumour from the LORD, and an ambassador is sent among the heathen, Arise ye, and let us rise up against her in battle.

2 Behold, I have made thee small among the heathen: thou art greatly despised.

3 The pride of thine heart hath deceived thee, thou that dwellest in the clefts of the rock, whose habitation is high; that saith in his heart, Who shall bring me down to the ground?

4 Though thou exalt thy self as the eagle, and though thou set thy nest among the stars, thence will I bring thee down, saith the LORD.

[5] If thieves came to thee, if robbers by night, (how art thou cut off!) would they not have stolen till they had enough? if the grape gatherers came to thee, would they not leave some grapes?

[6] How are the things of Esau searched out! How are his hidden things sought up!

[7] All the men of thy confederacy have brought thee even to the border: the men that were at peace with thee have deceived thee, and prevailed against thee; they that eat thy bread have laid a wound under thee: there is none understanding in him.

[8] Shall I not in that day, saith the LORD, even destroy the wise men out of Edom, and understanding out of the mount of Esau?"

Obadiah 1:1-8

So Esau is fitted for destruction. Both Him and all those that are with Him. They and the Gentiles make up the demon hoard that is attempting today to finish the job they began with the destruction of the Temple in 70 AD. It's the last sequel of the good vs. evil, Abba Yah vs. Satan movie. "Same ancient hatred, different day."

And so Black man, aka Negro, Slaves, Israelite, Hebrew, what's the answer? What are we going to do now?

The earth has been given into the hand of the wicked. Our open enemy controls everything. They control what we see, what we think, what we eat, what we buy, what we hear, and how we do what we do. Everything in our lives is under their control. All is lost, right? If we are to have anything, we must go to the

133

enemy on bent knee and beg them to have mercy on our poor wretched souls, right? I don't think so.

The Answer

Grand Rising

> 2And shalt return unto the LORD thy God...3That then the LORD thy God will turn thy captivity,...and will return and gather thee from all the nations,...5And the LORD thy God will bring thee into the land which thy fathers possessed,...and multiply thee above thy fathers. 6And the LORD thy God will circumcise thine heart, and the heart of thy seed, to love the LORD thy God with all thine heart...7And the LORD thy God will put all these curses upon thine enemies, and on them that hate thee, which persecuted thee.
>
> Deuteronomy 30:1-7

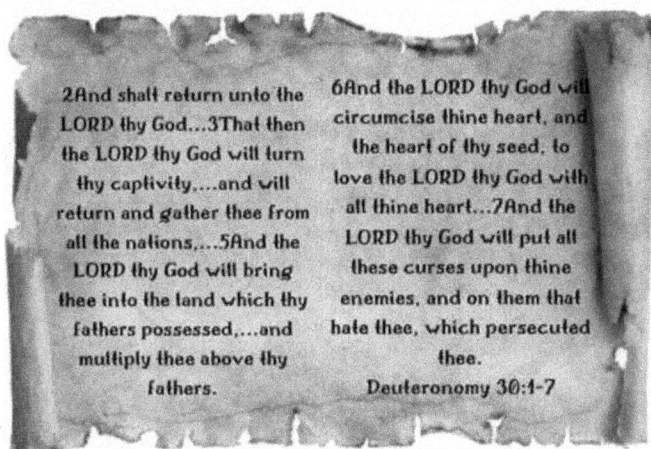

L et us start by making the main point of this book, and that is that the so-called Black man, aka Negroes are the true bloodline Israelites of the Tribe of Judah. And the ONLY way to put an end to our nightmare is to return to the Laws, Statutes, and Commands of our Elohim Yahuah T'Sebaoth.

"1 For, behold, in those days, and in that time, when I shall bring again the captivity of Judah and Jerusalem,

2 I will also gather all nations, and will bring them down into the valley of Jehoshaphat, and will plead with them there for My people and for My heritage Israel, whom they have scattered among the nations, and parted My land.

3 And they have cast lots for My people; and have given a boy for an harlot, and sold a girl for wine, that they might drink.

4 Yea, and what have ye to do with Me, O Tyre, and Zidon, and all the coasts of Palestine? will ye render Me a recompense? and if ye recompense Me, swiftly and speedily will I return your recompence upon your own head;

5 Because ye have taken My silver and My gold, and have carried into your temples My goodly pleasant things:

6 The children also of Judah and the children of Jerusalem have ye sold unto the Grecians, that ye might remove them far from their border.

7 Behold, I will raise them out of the place whither ye have sold them, and will return your recompence upon your own head:

8 And I will sell your sons and your daughters into the hand of the children of Judah, and they shall sell them to the Sabeans, to a people far off: for the LORD hath spoken it.

9 Proclaim ye this among the Gentiles; Prepare war, wake up the mighty men, let all the men of war draw near; let them come up:

10 Beat your plowshares into swords, and your pruninghooks into spears: let the weak say, I am strong.

11 Assemble yourselves, and come, all ye heathen, and gather yourselves together round about: thither cause thy mighty ones to come down, O LORD.

136

[12] Let the heathen be wakened, and come up to the valley of Jehoshaphat: for there will I sit to judge all the heathen round about."

Joel 3:1-12

The prophecy in Joel clearly tells us why ha'Maschiach is returning and who He is coming for. He is not coming for Gentiles, though they can and will be included in those that are saved. He is not coming for heathens even though they can and will be saved as long as they turn to ha'Maschiach (not fake white Jesus but that Negro who came out of the Tribe of Judah). And yes, Black man, aka Negro, Hebrews Israelite, you too cannot enter into the Kingdom unless you repent and accept your Kinsman Redeemer Yahshua ha'Maschiach. Just knowing that you are a Hebrew Israelite is not enough. You MUST return to His Laws, Statutes, and Commands as well as receive Him as Savior. He is coming for His people that went back into captivity one more time because our forefathers rejected Him.

There is a myriad of Scripture that confirms the identity of Israel's true descendants, aka the so-called Negroes, who have been carried away captive into all nations just as ha'Maschiach has said in Luke 21:23-24. As stated previously, no other people have been sent around the world as slaves other than the people who were in Jerusalem at the time that Yahshua made the prophetic statements of Luke 21,

137

"23 ...in those days! for there shall be great distress in the land, and wrath upon this people.

24 And they shall fall by the edge of the sword, and shall be led away captive into all nations:..."

Luke 21:23-24

Let's review again for the doubters. ONLY the so-called Negroes have been carried as slaves all over the world. Here's the list of places where we have been taken as slaves:

- Africa
- Middle East
- Europe
- North America
- The Islands
- Central America

- South America
- India
- China
- Australia
- Japan
- Indonesia

In all of these places, the so-called Negro, aka true descendants of Jacob, were taken as slaves. No other people as a people or group have ever been enslaved throughout the world. ONLY the Negro fits this prophecy. NO ONE ELSE FITS.

And Abba Yah uses this exact tool as punishment for His people, which He confirms in the very first sentence of Joel chapter 3. When we study the Old Testament, we see the same pattern repeated over and over again ad nauseam. Abba Yah blesses Israel. Israel sins against Abba Yah. He sends us into slavery. We cry out under the weight of oppression. He hears us. And comes to rescue us. We return to His Commandments and rejoice at His deliverance. Then we rinse and repeat. Only this time, THIS LAST TIME, the deliverance will be so vast as we can see from the remembrance of the Exodus of old,

"[14] Therefore, behold, the days come, saith the LORD, that it shall no more be said, The LORD liveth, that brought up the children of Israel out of the land of Egypt;

139

[15] But, The LORD LIVETH, THAT BROUGHT UP THE CHILDREN OF ISRAEL FROM THE LAND OF THE NORTH, and from all the lands whither He had driven them: and I will bring them again into their land that I gave unto their fathers."

Jeremiah 16:14-15

So, the coming deliverance of the children of Israel will be so great that no one will talk about the first Exodus any longer. Because it will encompass a people being gathered from all over the world who are being held captive across the globe,

"[30] For I knew that they would not hear Me, because it is a stiffnecked people: BUT IN THE LAND OF THEIR CAPTIVITIES THEY SHALL REMEMBER THEMSELVES.

[31] And shall know that I am the Lord their God: for I will give them an heart, and ears to hear:

[32] And they shall praise Me in the land of their captivity, and think upon My name,

[33] And return from their stiff neck, and from their wicked deeds: for they shall remember the way of their fathers, which sinned before the Lord.

[34] And I will bring them again into the land which I promised with an oath unto their fathers, Abraham, Isaac, and Jacob, and they shall be lords of it: and I will increase them, and they shall not be diminished.

[35] And I will make an everlasting covenant with them to be their God, and they shall be my people: and I will no more drive my people of Israel out of the land that I have given them."

Baruch 2:30-35

There are only one people on earth that are living in the land of their captivity, and that is the so-called Negroes. Everywhere we are found, we are still languishing at the bottom of society in

140

someone else's land. We are at the bottom, looking up everywhere we are found; whether you are part of the Siddi people of India or the Kunlun descendants of Chinese slaves or the Sanj of Saudi Arabia or Negroes of Brazil, or you name the areas where our people, the so-called Negroes are located. Even in the regions that are considered to be our own countries, we are at the bottom. In which African countries are the Seed of Israel (most of West and Southern Africa) actually running the country? Every head of state is hand-picked by Europeans (the seed of Satan) to preside over the people in a way that allows the seed of Satan to rape, rob, and pillage these countries. Dr. King said, "The Negro finds himself in exile in his own land." He was speaking of the Negroes in America, many of whom were the Natives that were here when the Europeans showed up. But the same script applies to the Bantu people in Africa. You can go to every country, and you will find the Europeans in control of the resources, followed by the East Indians or now the Chinese. So even in the lands we control, we are at the bottom of our own societies.

We hear and see shocking stories of Europeans and Asians abusing Africans, most of whom are Israelites (the Bantu people are actually Israelites), in their own land. We've all seen the video of the drunken white, aka European missionary, cursing and slapping around the African hotel worker. And these grown-ass men who with one punch could knock this crackka into the middle next week, are cowering before this fool because he says he looks like fake white Jesus. And then all of our people are praising our brothers for their restraint. What other people or government would tolerate such treatment of their people by foreigners in their own land?

But that's not enough; even the Chinese are getting into the act. There are daily stories of China men beating, pistol-whipping, and locking up our people, not in China but in Africa while not even being able to speak the local African language. How could this be? As Malcolm said, "It's the same game going all the time." Everywhere we are found, it's the same situation.

Could a Chinese man come to New York and start slapping around Americans? Could a European go to the Middle East and start beating around an Arab? Could an East Indian go to Japan and start slapping around the Japanese? It is not even a topic to be discussed.

So What We 'Gon Do?

In America, where police murder of so-called Negroes continues unabated, black murder porn is now a thing. Whether it be Breonna Taylor, Ahmad Aubrey, George Floyd, or countless other brothers or sisters in the US, murder of unarmed compliant Black folks is in vogue and has been for some time. There is some sort of ritualistic demonic spirit behind this blood lust. Meanwhile, the leaders in our community are once again reaching for the tried and true, marching, demonstrations, and begging our open enemy to please stop abusing, stealing, and killing us. They engage in midnight prayer sessions to pray that mercy be shown on our open enemies that only understand rape, robbery, and murder. However, the sad truth is that most Black Christian Pastors do absolutely nothing. In fact, they don't even mention it whatsoever. And the white Pastors tell us slavery was a good thing and say if you comply, nothing would happen. Tell that to Breonna Taylor, Botham "SHEM" Jean, Atatiana Jefferson, and Philando Castillo, just to name a few. Didn't He tell us that if we would not keep His Commands that,

> *"65 And among these nations shalt thou find no ease, neither shall the sole of thy foot have rest: but the LORD shall give thee there a trembling heart, and failing of eyes, and sorrow of mind:*
>
> *66 And thy life shall hang in doubt before thee; and thou shalt fear day and night, and shalt have none assurance of thy life:"*
>
> Deuteronomy 28:65-66

We have tried these methods over and over again. Europeans here in America continue to say it takes time to get to the point of fully embracing African Americans as equal in this society. Others have said it's all a figment of our imagination. And if we made a better effort at assimilation and stop complaining so much, things would be much better. However, after four hundred years of asking, begging, pleading with Europeans to treat us fairly and equally, it is time to stop and re-evaluate the situation.

We now know that the Black man, aka Negro, Israelite, Hebrew, are indeed the Chosen people of Abba Yah. So in light of that fact, how much sense does it make to keep going back to our open enemy to ask for fair and equal treatment? We are the seed of Yah, and the Europeans are the seed of Satan, as we have seen. These folks are our open enemy because they are the enemy of Abba Yah,

Malak Yesha'Yahu ben Yahudah

"1 {A Song or Psalm of Asaph.} Keep not Thou silence, O God: hold not Thy peace, and be not still, O God.

2 For, lo, Thine ENEMIES make a tumult: and they that hate Thee have lifted up the head.

3 They have taken crafty counsel against THY PEOPLE, and consulted against THY HIDDEN ONES.

4 They have said, Come, and let us cut them off from being a nation; that the name of Israel may be no more in remembrance.

5 For they have consulted together with one consent: they are confederate against thee:

6 The tabernacles of Edom, and the Ishmaelites; of Moab, and the Hagarenes;

7 Gebal, and Ammon, and Amalek; the Philistines with the inhabitants of Tyre;

8 Assur also is joined with them: they have holpen the children of Lot. Selah.

9 Do unto them as unto the Midianites; as to Sisera, as to Jabin, at the brook of Kison:

10 Which perished at Endor: they became as dung for the earth.

11 Make their nobles like Oreb, and like Zeeb: yea, all their princes as Zebah, and as Zalmunna:

12 Who said, Let us take to ourselves the Houses of God in possession.

13 O my God, make them like a wheel; as the stubble before the wind.

14 As the fire burneth a wood, and as the flame setteth the mountains on fire;

15 So persecute them with Thy tempest, and make them afraid with Thy storm.

145

⁶ Fill their faces with shame; that they may seek Thy name, O LORD.

¹⁷ Let them be confounded and troubled for ever; yea, let them be put to shame, and perish:

¹⁸ That men may know that Thou, whose name alone is JEHOVAH, art The Most High over all the earth."

Psalms 83

These, along with the Gentiles, whom Abba Yah has proclaimed Himself to be The Destroyer of the Gentiles, have made themselves our enemy, and by extension, they have made themselves enemies of The Most High (TMH),

"⁸ For thus saith the LORD of hosts; After the glory hath He sent me unto the nations which spoiled you: for he that toucheth you toucheth the apple of His eye."

Zechariah 2:8

We are the apple of TMH's eye, so any person that puts his or her hands on us will be in danger of His judgment. When you spend time studying the prophets of the Bible, you quickly realize that the true context of Scripture is that Abba Yah or TMH is ONLY speaking to His people from Genesis to Acts with a short detour to tell the Gentiles and the heathens that they too can enter into the Kingdom of Abba Yah as long as they cleave to Israel in the name of Yahshua ha'Maschiach and understand that the Kingdom of Yah is to Judah or the Yahudi first and then the Gentiles and everyone else,

"[1] For the LORD will have mercy on Jacob, and will yet choose Israel, and set them in their own land: and the strangers shall be joined with them, and they shall cleave to the house of Jacob.

[2] And the people shall take them, and bring them to their place: and the house of Israel shall possess them in the land of the LORD for servants and handmaids: and they shall take them captives, whose captives they were; and they shall rule over their oppressors."

Isaiah 14:1-2

Romans let us know that He has not cast away His people. And that the Gentiles have not replaced Israel as Western European Style Christianity tries to make us believe, but rather they will be grafted into the Kingdom, Yahudi first, then the Gentiles. And Paul even warned them not to boast against the Chosen of Yah,

"[18] Boast not against the branches. But if thou boast, thou bearest not the root, but the root thee.

[19] Thou wilt say then, The branches were broken off, that I might be graffed in.

[20] Well; because of unbelief they were broken off, and thou standest by faith. Be not highminded, but fear:

[21] For if God spared not the natural branches, take heed lest He also spare not thee.

[22] Behold therefore the goodness and severity of God: on them which fell, severity; but toward thee, goodness, if thou continue in His goodness: otherwise thou also shalt be cut off.

[23] And they also, if they abide not still in unbelief, shall be graffed in: for God is able to graff them in again.

[24] For if thou wert cut out of the olive tree which is wild by nature, and wert graffed contrary to nature into a good olive

147

tree: how much more shall these, which be the natural branches, be graffed into their own olive tree?"

Romans 11:18-24

So the Scripture is clear that true Israel has not been done away with, and in fact, Abba Yah goes on to say He is bringing us back,

> *"25 For I would not, brethren, that ye should be ignorant of this mystery, lest ye Should be wise in your own conceits; that blindness in part is happened to Israel, until the fulness of the Gentiles be come in.*
>
> *26 And so all Israel shall be saved: as it is written, There shall come out of Sion the Deliverer, and shall turn away ungodliness from Jacob:*
>
> *27 For this is My Covenant unto them, when I shall take away their sins."*
>
> *Romans 11:25-27*

The problem for the seed of Satan is that just like their father, they want to be at the head. Wasn't it Satan that said,

> *"13 For thou hast said in thine heart, I will ascend into heaven, I will exalt my throne above the stars of God: I will sit also upon the mount of the congregation, in the sides of the north:*
>
> *14 I will ascend above the heights of the clouds; I will be like the most High."*
>
> *Isaiah 14:13-14*

So these fools want to exalt themselves above the God of all creation. And if they cannot reign there, they will try to reign over His people. This is why it matters who Abba Yah's people are. Even Hitler said that these fools are planning to take on God Himself. Whether we like it or not, know it or not or understand it or not, we are at war with a people led by the chief of their armies, the imposters in Israel whose sole mission and desire is to take on Abba Yah. And to that, we say, Yahuah T'Sebaoth. The Scripture says,

"3 The LORD is a man of war: the LORD is His name."

Exodus 15:3

We are His men of war, and both the men and women of Israel are in this together. When Sarah kicked Hagar out of the house, it was her giving Abraham the backup he didn't know he needed. Abraham had a soft spot in his heart for Ishmael, but he wasn't the seed of promise. When Rebecca was faced with the decision of whether or not to stand by and allow the destiny of our forefathers to be in the hands of Esau (whom Abba Yah hated then and still hates to this day), she was working in favor of Abraham. Abba Yah took action and saved ALL of mankind from a fate worse than death. And that is to put the destiny of the entire planet in the hands of the wicked, which is Esau, aka Europeans, fake Jews. These are the seed of Satan that Yahshua ha'Maschiach is coming back to destroy.

So Black man whatcha 'gon do? Shoot or dribble? You 'gon wake up and live up to your calling as prophesied in Ezekiel 37,

"⁵ Thus saith the Lord GOD unto these bones; Behold, I will cause breath to enter into you, and ye shall live:..

¹⁰ So I prophesied as He commanded me, and the breath came into them, and they lived, and stood up upon their feet, an exceeding great army."

Ezekiel 37:5,10

He has given us His breath to use His Word to bring down this beast system as His exceedingly great army. The prophets are back in the land spiritually speaking. Or, are you going to continue this foolishness of marching, begging, and bowing down to your open enemy, hoping, and praying that somehow 'Ole Massa 'gon hear you and somehow find it in his heart to treat you right?

We have been doing that for 400 years. How much closer are we to equal treatment than we were when we started? NOT ONE STEP CLOSER. We are frozen in place, and the only way out is straight ahead in the power of The Most High (TMH), Yahuah T'Sebaoth. But how do we go forward in the power of TMH? We live in a society where there are over 350,000,000 weapons in the hands of white America all pointed at you, NEGRO. They have shown that they have no problem pulling the trigger. So are we to believe that we can join up with the No Fucking Around Crew, NFAC? Really? Between them, there may be 100,000 weapons. Don't get me wrong, I salute the willingness to confront the seed of Satan head-on without fear, but what did our Yahuah tell us to do, and what has been His history?

"2 But I beseech you, that I may not be bold when I am present with that confidence, wherewith I think to be bold against some, which think of us as if we walked according to the flesh.

3 For though we walk in the flesh, we do not war after the flesh:

4 (For the weapons of our warfare are not carnal, but mighty through God to the pulling down of strong holds;)

5 Casting down imaginations, and every high thing that exalteth itself against the knowledge of God, and bringing into captivity every thought to the obedience of Christ;

6 And having in a readiness to revenge all disobedience, when your obedience is fulfilled."

2 Corinthians 10:2-6

No shade to the NFAC, but your weapons are no match for a country full of people that hate you and all Negroes because they hate Abba Yah Himself and the true Son of God Yahshua ha'Maschiach. In fact, they hate TMH so much that they changed His image into a likeness of themselves as the Scripture said they would,

"48 And laid open the book of the law, wherein the heathen had sought to paint the likeness of their images."

1 Maccabees 3:48

So these carnal weapons are of no consequence, UNLESS they are anointed of Yahuah T'Sebaoth, aka Abba Yah, TMH. And we don't have to look far to see the effect of His handy work. This entire awakening is the result of TMH using the world's foolish things to bring this entire nation and world to its knees with a coronavirus.

Consider that Abba Yah has used the likes of Oswald Bates from In Living Color that made no sense when speaking in his carnal mind. These same men have now become the prophets on the street corner in power ranger outfits (their words not mine), speaking forth the true Besorah under the power of the Holy Spirit or Ruach ha'Kodesh. These brothers deliver more truth and more Word on the street corner than the stadium-filled televangelists have ever delivered, combined, even when you throw in their multi-million dollar jets and mansions. Why is that?

It's because they are not telling people the truth. And the fundamental Biblical truth is that:

Abba Yah is Black

His Son is Black

His Chosen people are Black

His Chosen people are Black

These brothers on the street corner who have received the "breath" spoken of in Ezekiel 37 are responsible for awakening the true children of Israel to their lost heritage and unleashing upon the earth that exceeding great army that was prophesied by Yahuah T'Sebaoth. It is these brothers that have brought this world into disarray, backed up by assemblies quietly coming together into the unity of the faith to proclaim the true Gospel, the true Besorah of Yahshua ha'Maschiach that tells us that He is ONLY coming for Israel and those non-Israelites who cleave to Israel.

We can only do the impossible, which is bringing down this world system of oppression by returning to our Super Power which is the keeping His Laws, Statutes, and Commands. Our God, our Elohim, is not about equality. He is about rulership. And we, the so-called Negroes, aka Israelites, Hebrews, are the people He has chosen to rule and reign with Yahshua ha'Maschiach when He returns. In every army, in every Kingdom, in every family, and in every company, there is a hierarchy. There is the leader or king, then the generals, then the captains, and then the soldiers. Likewise, in the Kingdom of our Elohim to come, Yahshua ha'Maschiach is our king, the twelve Apostles are the generals, the prophets are the captains, and the rest of the Chosen are the soldiers that will carry out the Word of TMH. The heathens, the Gentiles, and the strangers will be our servants in the coming Kingdom of Yah.

153

This is the John 3:16 everyone keeps referring to:

"16 For God so loved the world, that He gave His only begotten Son, that whosoever believeth in Him should not perish, but have everlasting life.

17 For God sent not His Son into the world to condemn the world; but that the world through Him might be saved."

John 3:16-17

This is the world that TMH gave His Son for. This is the world that Yahshua ha'Maschiach gave His life for, not the world that was given into the hand of the wicked as spoken of in Job,

"24 The earth is given into the hand of the wicked: he covereth the faces of the judges thereof; if not, where, and who is he?"

Job 9:24

He gave His life for the world to come, not for the world that is. Those people, the wicked people, aka the Europeans and those that are confederate with them, are the seed of Satan who will bow before the King of Kings and the Lord of Lords along with the true children of Israel whom they held in derision.

We can ONLY come into our true selves, our true power, by coming back to Yahuah T'Sebaoth and His Laws, Statutes, and Commands in the name of our King Yahshua ha'Maschiach. He never promised you equality; He promised you and all Israel, aka Negroes, rulership through the Covenant that He affirmed in

Abraham and reaffirmed in both the Old Testament and the New Testament.

The Covenant,

"13 And He said unto Abram, Know of a surety that thy seed shall be a stranger in a land that is not theirs, and shall serve them; and they shall afflict them four hundred years;

14 And also that nation, whom they shall serve, will I judge: and afterward shall they come out with great substance.

15 And thou shalt go to thy fathers in peace; thou shalt be buried in a good old age.

16 But in the fourth generation they shall come hither again: for the iniquity of the Amorites is not yet full."

Genesis 15:13-16

The Reaffirmation,

"31 Behold, the days come, saith the LORD, that I will make a New Covenant with the House of Israel, and with the House of Judah:

32 Not according to the Covenant that I made with their fathers in the day that I took them by the hand to bring them out of the land of Egypt; which My Covenant they brake, although I was an Husband unto them, saith the LORD:

33 But this shall be the Covenant that I will make with the House of Israel; After those days, saith the LORD, I will put My law in their inward parts, and write it in their hearts; and will be their God, and they shall be My people."

Jeremiah 31:31-33

And,

"7 For if that first Covenant had been faultless, then should no place have been sought for the second.

8 For finding fault with them, He saith, Behold, the days come, saith the Lord, when I will make a New Covenant with the House of Israel and with the House of Judah:

9 Not according to the covenant that I made with their fathers in the day when I took them by the hand to lead them out of the land of Egypt; because they continued not in My Covenant, and I regarded them not, saith the Lord.

10 For this is the Covenant that I will make with the House of Israel after those days, saith the Lord; I will put My laws into their mind, and write them in their hearts: and I will be to them a God, and they shall be to Me a people:"

Hebrews 8:8-10

The Rulership,

"1 And it shall come to pass, if thou shalt hearken diligently unto the voice of the LORD thy God, to observe and to do all His Commandments which I command thee this day, that the LORD thy God will SET THEE ON HIGH ABOVE ALL NATIONS of the earth:

2 And all these blessings shall come on thee, and overtake thee, if thou shalt hearken unto the voice of the LORD thy God."

Deuteronomy 28:1-2

And

> *"⁹ Tribulation and anguish, upon every soul of man that doeth evil, of the Jew first, and also of the Gentile;*
>
> *¹⁰ But glory, honour, and peace, to every man that worketh good, to the Jew first, and also to the Gentile:*
>
> *¹¹ For there is no respect of persons with God."*
>
> Romans 2:9-11

Our Elohim is no respecter of persons, but He is the God of order:

1. Yahuah, the Creator
2. Yahshua ha'Maschiach, the Son
3. Israel, His Chosen people
4. Gentiles, heathens and strangers, the servants

Ain't Nothin' Like the Real Thing, Baby

Now back to the sisters, the Ema's, the Achoti. We are ALL, Hebrew man, woman, and child in this together. There is no one else with us. Everyone else has stood by and watched and even participated in our destruction. And TMH is sending His Son back to destroy them. We must huddle together in the Spirit against the seed of Satan and those that are confederate against us who are our open enemy. And we need our women to have our back even when we don't see it. Rebecca saw what Isaac didn't see. That is why TMH forbade Israel to mix with these other nations' women because they cannot see what our Achoti

158

and Ema's see. Maybe I missed something, but which one of these Gentile, heathen or strange women ever gave Israel proper direction? Solomon had a thousand wives and concubines from all these other nations, and they led him astray. In this battle, Abba Yah said,

> *"28 And it shall come to pass afterward, that I will pour out My spirit upon all flesh; and your sons and your daughters shall prophesy, your old men shall dream dreams, your young men shall see visions:*
>
> *29 And also upon the servants and upon the handmaids in those days will I pour out my spirit."*

Joel 2:28-29

If we are honest, no other woman has done for Israel what the daughters of Zion have done. If we were ineffective as a unit, they would not have invested so heavily in trying to break us apart. Do they teach Asian women, "You don't need a man?"

Did they tell any other group of people that the one condition for receiving government benefits is that there can be NO man in the house?

The only family unit the seed of Satan has ever focused on destroying is the Black, aka Hebrew Israelite Family. Why is that?

Because they know and understand that the so-called Negroes are the true Hebrews. They know that when true Israel

159

comes to themselves, it's game over. They know that once we realize who we are and return to our Elohim and His Commands, they are in trouble. As the Scripture declares,

> *"⁷ Behold, I will raise them out of the place whither ye have sold them…"*

Joel 3:7

Oh devil, you in trouble now, for we are the sons of the True and Living Elohim who have returned in the power and might of the Son of The Most High to reclaim the Throne.

There is no need for a substitute when the real people are still on the earth, and Abba Yah makes it clear through the mouth of ha'Maschiach that He came to seek and save that which was lost. It is the false Western European Style Christianity that says Israel will be replaced when Abba Yah says in the end-time battle that Satan goes off to make war against the seed of the woman who is true Israel,

> *"¹⁷ And the dragon was wroth with the woman, and went to make war with the remnant of her seed, which keep the Commandments of God, and have the testimony of Jesus Christ."*

Revelation 12:17

The Destroyer of the Gentiles is on His Way

Are those in Israel today the ones that have the testimony of Yahshua? Once again, it is the Scripture that identifies who is who, not the traditions and commandments of men. When ha'Maschiach returns, He will crack the skies riding a white horse with His garment dipped in the blood of those that make war with the seed of the woman and oppose the Father and His Laws, Statutes, and Commands. Right now, as we speak, the Gentiles are celebrating their new Space Force that they claim will help them establish supremacy in the skies. The US is leading the effort and, in their own words, state what the objective is and the reason they need to militarize the skies:

Q: What is the U.S. Space Force (USSF)?

A: The USSF is the newest branch of the Armed Forces. It was established on December 20, 2019 with the enactment of the Fiscal Year 2020 National Defense Authorization Act and will be stood-up over the next 18 months.

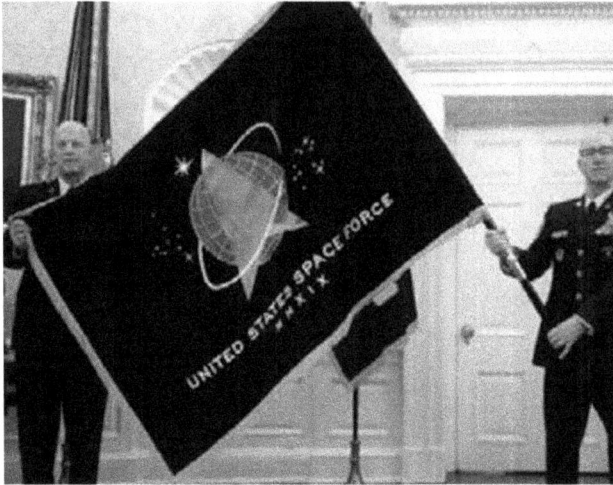

Q: What is the mission of the U.S. Space Force?

A: The U.S. Space Force is a military service that organizes, trains, and equips space forces in order to protect U.S. and allied interests in space and to provide space capabilities to the joint force. USSF responsibilities will include developing military space professionals, acquiring military space systems, maturing the military doctrine for space power, and organizing space forces to present to our Combatant Commands.

Q: Why do we need a Space Force?

A: Space has become essential to our security and prosperity – so much so that we need a branch of our military dedicated to its defense, just like we have branches of the military dedicated to protecting and securing the air, land, and sea. Unfettered access to space is vital to national defense. Space systems are woven into the fabric of our way of life. Space affects almost every part of our daily lives and is fundamental to our economic system. For example, satellites not only power the GPS technology that we use daily, but allow us to surf the web and call our friends, enable first responders to communicate with each other in times of crisis, time-stamp transactions in the world financial market, and even allow us to use credit cards at gas pumps. (source - spaceforce.mil)

These same people have been working on the CERN Project (Conseil Européen pour la Recherche Nucléaire or European Council for Nuclear Research), whose real goal is to attempt to establish a portal that would allow them to reach into the spiritual dimension and communicate directly with their god, Satan. The stated goals are innocuous and designed as always to make the evil look and sound beneficial.

So what's the point? Notice that these are all European nations working together to fulfill the work of Satan as pointed out in Revelation 12,

> *"17 And the dragon was wroth with the woman, and went to make war with the remnant of her seed..."*
>
> *Revelation 12:17*

When we look at the nations behind this project, we see that they are ALL European:

- Austria
- Belgium
- Bulgaria
- Czech Republic
- Denmark
- Finland
- France
- Germany
- Greece
- Hungary
- Israel
- Italy
- Netherlands
- Norway
- Poland
- Portugal
- Romania
- Serbia
- Slovakia
- Spain
- Sweden

- Switzerland

- United Kingdom

The USA is left out of this list, but they are walking in lockstep with their European allies. Noticeably absent is any black nation. Now, why is that? Could it be that we are the seed of the woman whose job is to oppose the enemies of Abba Yah and His Son, our Kinsman Redeemer?

Doesn't the Scripture say,

> *"[19] And I will give unto thee the keys of the kingdom of heaven: and whatsoever thou shalt bind on earth shall be bound in heaven: and whatsoever thou shalt loose on earth shall be loosed in heaven."*

> *Matthew 16:19*

Could it be that we are here on earth as the seed of the woman to agree with that which is said in the heavenlies? As has been stated all along, Abba Yah has a seed in the earth realm and Satan has a seed. This is the ancient battle that began with Cain and Abel and continued on through Jacob and Esau and will play itself out through these same two nations of people,

> *"[9] For Esau is the end of the world, and Jacob is the beginning of it that followeth."*

> *2 Esdras 6:9*

And just for the uninitiated among us, let us review this. Edom, which are descendants of Esau, were attacked and

165

defeated by Kittim, which is Romim, which is Rome. The Romans swallowed up the children of Edom and they became part of the Roman Empire. These Edomites have been folded into the European nations and eventually became the white Jews we see today, especially those that have very curly hair. But don't get it twisted; much of Esau is still black and still in Africa.

Now, back to the lecture at hand, the two seeds. The seed of satan is manifested in these European people that cannot live in peace and harmony with anyone, anywhere, at anytime. Even when we attempt to live at peace with them, they simply cannot help themselves. They must kill, steal, and destroy, which is evidenced by the myriad of black (read Hebrew Israelites) men and women who are almost always shot and killed by police while posing absolutely no threat. These murderers are the people Yahshua ha'Maschiach is coming back to destroy,

> *"¹ Who is this that cometh from Edom, with dyed garments from Bozrah? this that is glorious in His apparel, travelling in the greatness of His strength? I that speak in righteousness, mighty to save.*
>
> *² Wherefore art Thou red in Thine apparel, and Thy garments like him that treadeth in the winefat?*
>
> *³ I have trodden the winepress alone; and of the people there was none with Me: for I will tread them in Mine anger, and trample them in My fury; and their blood shall be sprinkled upon My garments, and I will stain all My raiment.*
>
> *⁴ For the day of vengeance is in Mine heart, and the year of My redeemed is come.*

⁵ And I looked, and there was none to help; and I wondered that there was none to uphold: therefore Mine own arm brought salvation unto Me; and My fury, it upheld Me.

⁶ And I will tread down the people in Mine anger, and make them drunk in My fury, and I will bring down their strength to the earth."

Isaiah 63:1-6

As always in the mouth of two or three witnesses, let every Word be confirmed. The New Testament confirms what was said by the prophet Isaiah,

"¹¹ And I saw heaven opened, and behold a white horse; and He that sat upon him was called Faithful and True, and in righteousness He doth judge and make war.

¹² His eyes were as a flame of fire, and on His head were many crowns; and He had a name written, that no man knew, but He Himself.

¹³ And He was clothed with a vesture dipped in blood: and His name is called The Word of God.

¹⁴ And the armies which were in heaven followed Him upon white horses, clothed in fine linen, white and clean.

¹⁵ And out of His mouth goeth a sharp sword, that with it He should smite the nations: and He shall rule them with a rod of iron: and He treadeth the winepress of the fierceness and wrath of Almighty God. 16 And He hath on His vesture and on His thigh a name written, KING OF KINGS, AND LORD OF LORDS."

Revelation 19:11-16

Who are these people that Yahshua is coming back to destroy? His enemies, of course. Who has He called His enemies? Let's go down the list.

"¹³ As it is written, Jacob have I loved, but Esau have I hated."

Romans 9:13

"⁹ Behold, I will make them of the synagogue of Satan, which say they are Jews, and are not, but do lie; behold, I will make them to come and worship before thy feet, and to know that I have loved thee."

Revelation 3:9

"⁵ Therefore thus saith the Lord GOD; Surely in the fire of My jealousy have I spoken against the residue of the heathen, and against all Idumea, which have appointed My land into their possession with the joy of all their heart, with despiteful minds, to cast it out for a prey."   *Ezekiel 36:5*

"⁷ The lion is come up from his thicket, and the destroyer of the Gentiles is on His way..."

Jeremiah 4:7

"¹ And the word of the LORD came unto me, saying

² Son of man, set thy face against Gog, the land of Magog, the chief prince of Meshech and Tubal, and prophesy against him,

³ And say, Thus saith the Lord GOD; Behold, I am against thee, O Gog, the chief prince of Meshech and Tubal:"

Ezekiel 38:1-3

"⁶⁸ And the LORD shall bring thee into Egypt again with ships, by the way whereof I spake unto thee, Thou shalt see it no more again: and there ye shall be sold unto your enemies for bondmen and bondwomen, and no man shall buy you."

Deuteronomy 28:68

"⁸ For thus saith the LORD of hosts; After the glory hath He sent me unto the nations which spoiled you: for he that toucheth you toucheth the apple of His eye."

Zechariah 2:8

When you go through and study, you find that Abba Yah is against those that have abused His people, and He is sending His Son back to destroy those that have destroyed His people. As we have seen, the Europeans are the seed of Satan who comes from the north where Satan dwells.

What did Abba Yah say about Satan?

> *"¹¹ Thy pomp is brought down to the grave, and the noise of thy viols: the worm is spread under thee, and the worms cover thee.*
>
> *¹² How art thou fallen from heaven, O Lucifer, son of the morning! How art thou cut down to the ground, which didst weaken the nations!*
>
> *¹³ For thou hast said in thine heart, I will ascend into heaven, I will exalt my throne above the stars of God: I will sit also upon the mount of the congregation, in the sides of the north:*
>
> *¹⁴ I will ascend above the height of the clouds; I will be like The Most High.*
>
> *¹⁵ Yet thou shalt be brought down to hell, to the sides of the pit."*
>
> *Isaiah 14:11-15*

And,

> *"¹³ I know thy works, and where thou dwellest, even where Satan's seat is: and thou holdest fast My name, and hast not denied My faith, even in those days wherein Antipas was My faithful martyr, who was slain among you, where Satan dwelleth."*
>
> *Revelation 2:13*

By the way, who are the people that occupy the land of the north? Is it not the Europeans (who are a mixture of Esau,

Japheth, and the fallen angels)? These are the people to whom Abba Yah says He has indignation against forever. Why? Because they have shed the innocent blood of Israel,

> *"¹⁹ Egypt shall be a desolation, and Edom shall be a desolate wilderness, for the violence against the children of Judah, because they have shed innocent blood in their land.*
>
> *²⁰ But Judah shall dwell for ever, and Jerusalem from generation to generation.*
>
> *²¹ For I will cleanse their blood that I have not cleansed: for the LORD dwelleth in Zion."*   Joel 3:19-21

The Final Solution

On some level, we have been stricken, smitten of Yah, and afflicted just like our Kinsman Redeemer Yahshua ha'Maschiach. The difference is that we are guilty on all charges. He came ONLY for the lost sheep of the House of Israel. And yet we rejected Him, thereby earning every curse that has come our way. Surely we should be cast aside in favor of these other nations who have sought to steal our identity. But rather than recognize Abba Yah's Chosen people, they not only have sought to replace us, but they have sought to replace Abba Yah too by putting another Elohim and another ha'Maschiach on the Throne. One made in their earthly pagan image and their own earthly pagan's likeness.

Their god is one that kills, steals, and destroys the people of earth. Yahshua said, 'know them by their fruit,' and their fruit is rape, murder, death, and destruction everywhere they go. When they showed up in Africa, they took the people of Yah all over the world as slaves. Killing tens of millions in the process. When they showed up in the Western Hemisphere by their own admission, they slaughtered upwards of one hundred million of the inhabitants that were here. But they are not in this all alone. There are the white Arabs who have inherited the practice of enslaving the children of Israel in their own slave trade. They say that the Koran gives them license to continue the practice of slavery even to this day. Right now, as we speak, OPEN AIR SLAVE MARKETS are being conducted in Libya where ONLY the sons of Jacob are being enslaved. They are enticing young women from the African continent to come as domestic servants to these Middle Eastern countries to work, only to be enslaved once they get there. As our esteemed brother Professor John Henrik Clarke said, "The Negro does not have any friends on this earth." Dr. Clarke was right then, and he is right now. We continue to make the mistake of thinking we have friends that we do not have.

When selling us into slavery, the Arabs said, 'It's ok to enslave these people because they are cursed by their God.' That was correct. We were the ones that rejected the Laws, Statutes, and Commands of Yahuah our Elohim (God) the Creator of all things so that we might bow down to the false gods of wood (Western European Style Christian wooden cross) and stone (the Kabbalah stone of Mecca). These are gods of other nations that acknowledge that our Elohim is the one true and living God even in their founding documents. These nations and their gods have been confederate against the true bloodline descendants of Abraham, Isaac, and Jacob to hide our identity from the rest of the world as written in Psalms 83.

But now we are at the end. When Daniel went to write down the rest of the vision, the angel told him to seal up those words until the time of the end,

> *"¹ And at that time shall Michael stand up, the great prince which standeth for the children of thy people: and there shall be a time of trouble, such as never was since there was a nation even to that same time: and at that time thy people shall be delivered, every one that shall be found written in the book.*
>
> *² And many of them that sleep in the dust of the earth shall awake, some to everlasting life, and some to shame and everlasting contempt. 3 And they that be wise shall shine as the brightness of the firmament; and they that turn many to righteousness as the stars for ever and ever. 4 But thou, O Daniel, shut up the words, and seal the book, even to the time of the end: many shall run to and fro, and knowledge shall be increased."*
>
> *Daniel 12:1-4*

And that which has been hidden is being brought back to light. The war of the worlds is set to begin. This is what is meant by,

> *"16 Abba Yah so loved the world that He gave His only begotten Son."*
>
> *John 3:16*

He didn't give Yahshua for this world which has been given into the hand of the wicked as Job 9:24 says. Satan correctly said to ha'Maschiach that he is the ruler of this world because of the sin of Adam and Eve when they bit into the fruit from the forbidden tree,

> *5 And the devil, taking Him up into an high mountain, shewed unto Him all the kingdoms of the world in a moment of time.*
>
> *6 And the devil said unto Him, All this power will I give Thee, and the glory of them: for that is delivered unto me; and to whomsoever I will give it.*
>
> *7 If thou therefore wilt worship me, all shall be Thine.*
>
> *8 And Jesus answered and said unto him, Get thee behind Me, satan: for it is written, thou shalt worship the Lord thy God, and Him only shalt thou serve.*
>
> *Luke 4:5-8*

The world that Yahshua was referring to was not the world we are living in today, but rather the world that is to come where His Son will reign with a rod of iron for a thousand years before satan is loosed one last time to go and deceive the nations.

173

All of those that have opposed and hated true Israel and by extension the True and Living Elohim will go into captivity for that final one thousand years before Satan, and all those that agree with him are cast into the lake of fire where they will burn in everlasting fire forever and ever.

So what does this mean for the so-called Black Man, aka Niggers, Negroes, Israelites, Hebrews that have been scattered to all the earth? It means that the veil has been lifted off our eyes so that now we can see Satan and his anti-Christ and his people for who they are. Because of our fall, the earth has been in the hands of the wicked since at least 325 AD when Constantine accepted Yahshua ha'Maschiach and immediately changed the Holy to profane by giving us pagan holidays in place of Abba Yah's appointed Holy Days. They gave us Easter and Christmas and another savior that they eventually renamed Jesus instead of Yahshua ha'Maschiach. This false savior came for everybody and made Gentiles the replacement for Abba Yah's people. No such thing ever happened. Even Paul said,

> "[1] I say then, Hath God cast away His people? God forbid. For I also am an Israelite, of the seed of Abraham, of the tribe of Benjamin.
>
> [2] God hath not cast away his people which he foreknew. Wot ye not what the scripture saith of Elias? how he maketh intercession to God against Israel, saying,
>
> [3] Lord, they have killed thy prophets, and digged down thine altars; and I am left alone, and they seek my life.

174

[4](4) But what saith the answer of God unto him? I have reserved to myself seven thousand men, who have not bowed the knee to the image of Baal.

[5](5) Even so then at this present time also there is a remnant according to the election of grace.

[6](6) And if by grace, then is it no more of works: otherwise grace is no more grace. But if it be of works, then is it no more grace: otherwise work is no more work."

Romans 11:1-6

The awakened Hebrew Israelite is that remnant that Paul spoke about. However, being awake is only the beginning of the journey, not the end. Black man (and Black woman), you are true Israel, and as such, we must come back to His Laws, Statutes, and Commands. Most will argue that this is not so. We no longer need to keep the Law. Some Black Pastors have even suggested that keeping the Law is a sin. No shade to those Pastors but consider this.

Our people have kept fake white Jesus' doctrine since we got off the plantation, and yet our people are still being gunned down like dogs in the street by the descendants of those same European plantation owners that make towering glowing speeches about the brotherhood of man and how all mankind was made of one blood. And how we are all one in Christ. As Malcolm said,

"They may talk about brotherhood on Sunday but they don't practice it on NO day."

Consider that the Pastor told us that we could eat anything we like. Just pray over it in Jesus' name, and you'll be fine, yet the Black people in America are the sickest people around. And almost all of our illnesses are environmentally related. This is French for the food that we eat, which is unclean, is killing us. Now, Abba Yah told us not to eat unclean foods, but we eat them anyway, and we are sick while the Gentiles eat these things and are completely unaffected. Could this be another breadcrumb along the King's Highway leading us back to His Commands?

Consider that Massa offered us a seat at his table. But Massa's table is polluted with every wind of doctrine that is in direct opposition to the Word of Abba Yah. The seat at Massa's table is the removal of our God for that of an image of maniacal murdering, incestuous homosexual named Cesare Borgia cast as the image of the Son of Yahuah, Yahshua ha'Maschiach. At Massa's table, our place is one of servitude and oppression to a people that Abba Yah calls His enemy and our enemy.

As was said before, Dr. King said, "I fear I may have integrated my people into a burning house." Perhaps TMH revealed to Him who these so-called Christians and fake jews really were. Shortly afterward, he tried to pivot the poor people's campaign where he said, "We're coming to Washington to get our check." Understanding that the jig was up or soon would be if he stayed on the Poor People's campaign rhetoric, he was assassinated by these same people that profess love for Abba Yah, but secretly plot to keep us in subjection to them and their wicked ways,

"3 The wicked are estranged from the womb: they go astray as soon as they be born, speaking lies."

Psalms 58:3

Come Out From Among Them

Consider that Yahshua ha'Maschiach said,

"4 And I heard another voice from heaven, saying, Come out of her, My people, that ye be not partakers of her sins, and that ye receive not of her plagues."

Revelation 18:4

But how do we come out from among them? We come out from Babylon by returning to our Elohim's Laws, Statutes, and Commands. Following TMH is the only way out.

Yet we have made it our business to follow the ways of oppressors and we are still at the bottom of society no matter how hard we try to follow in their footsteps. Could it be that our power ONLY comes from following the Laws, Statutes, and Commands of our Elohim, Abba Yah, who once again said,

"¹ And it shall come to pass, if thou shalt hearken diligently unto the voice of the LORD thy God, to observe and to do all His commandments which I command thee this day, that the LORD thy God will set thee on high above all nations of the earth:

² And all these blessings shall come on thee, and overtake thee, if thou shalt hearken unto the voice of the LORD thy God."

Deuteronomy 28:1-2

We have been fed a web of lies that tells us that God loves everyone when He spent the entirety of the Old Testament telling us that we are the apple of His eye and how much He valued us above all people on the earth,

"⁵⁶ As for the other people which also come of Adam, Thou hast said that they are nothing, but be like unto spittle, and hast likened the abundance of them unto a drop that falleth from a vessell."

2 Esdras 6:56

And then in the New Testament, He continued to say, "To Yahuda first then the Gentiles."

The nations have invested heavily in keeping us away from our power which is the keeping of Abba Yahs Laws, Statutes, and Commands. The keeping of His Laws is our SUPERPOWER. Consider again Deuteronomy 28:1,

"¹...observe and to do all His commandments which I command thee this day, that the LORD thy God WILL SET THEE ON HIGH ABOVE ALL NATIONS OF THE EARTH:"

178

When we see Israel flowing in the light of Abba Yah's Word, we are NEVER defeated. We perform superhuman feats. How does Samson take the jawbone of an ass and strike down one thousand men with it? The only way this could happen is that Abba Yah's hand was on him.

Consider David going against Goliath. While all of his brothers were in fear, David stepped forward and said to Goliath,

> "*45 Thou comest to me with a sword, and with a spear, and with a shield: but I come to thee in the name of the LORD of hosts (Yahuah T'Sebaoth), the God of the armies of Israel, whom thou hast defied.*
>
> *46 This day will the LORD deliver thee into mine hand; and I will smite thee, and take thine head from thee; and I will give the carcases of the host of the Philistines this day unto the fowls of the air, and to the wild beasts of the earth; that all the earth may know that there is a God in Israel.*
>
> *47 And all this assembly shall know that the LORD saveth not with sword and spear: for the battle is the LORD'S, and he will give you into our hands.*"
>
> *1 Samuel 17:45-47*

Consider Shadrach, Meschach, and Abednego (otherwise known as Shadrach, Meschach and you bad Negroes) who; when King Nebuchadnezzar threatened their lives said,

> "*16 O Nebuchadnezzar, we are not careful to answer thee in this matter.*
>
> *17 If it be so, our God whom we serve is able to deliver us from the burning fiery furnace, and he will deliver us out of thine hand, O king.*

179

¹⁸ But if not, be it known unto thee, O king, that we will not serve thy gods, nor worship the golden image which thou hast set up."

Daniel 3:16-18

The story continued, and the King threw the Hebrew Israelites into the furnace. Yet they were not burned but walked around in the fire with One like unto the Son of man,

"²⁸ Then Nebuchadnezzar spake, and said, Blessed be the God of Shadrach, Meshach, and Abednego, who hath sent His angel, and delivered His servants that trusted in Him, and have changed the king's word, and yielded their bodies, that they might not serve nor worship any god, except their own God.

²⁹ Therefore I make a decree, That every people, nation, and language, which speak anything amiss against the God of Shadrach, Meshach, and Abednego, shall be cut in pieces, and their houses shall be made a dunghill: because THERE IS NO OTHER GOD THAT CAN DELIVER AFTER THIS SORT."

Daniel 3:28-29

Notice, if you will, the emphasis on the word "SAID;" in each case, something was said. And that which was said agreed with the Word and the Spirit of The Most High.

You see Black man, our power is wrapped up in the Covenant that we have with YAHUAH T'SEBAOTH. When we walk in Covenant with our God, our Elohim, are we perfect? Absolutely not. After all, He said,

"²² But the scripture hath concluded all under sin, that the promise by faith of Jesus Christ might be given to them that believe."

Galatians 3:22

Yahshua, Himself, said,

> *"[17] Why callest thou Me good? there is none good but One, that is, God: but if thou wilt enter into life, KEEP THE COMMANDMENTS."*

Matthew 19:17

So here we have ha'Maschiach in the New Testament saying, keep the Law. But again, because we have been exposed to Western European Style Christianity where we have been misled into thinking we were Gentiles, we thought that Abba Yah did away with the Law. Nothing could be further from the truth. We are true Israel, and nowhere in Scripture are the true children of Israel told not to keep the Law. In the book of Revelation, in several places, it tells us to keep the Law, most notably at the very end,

> *"[17] And the dragon was wroth with the woman, and went to make war with the remnant of her seed, WHICH KEEP THE COMMANDMENTS OF GOD and have the testimony of Jesus Christ."* *Revelation 12:17*

And,

> *"[14] Blessed are they that do HIS COMMANDMENTS, that they may have right to the tree of life, and may enter in through the gates into the city."*

Revelation 22:14

181

And so all this time, it has been the seed of Satan that has been working to keep us blind to who we are. They know in the halls of demonic power that their ONLY power is to keep us away from our knowledge of self and the reconnecting of ourselves to our power, our Elohim Yahuah, and His Laws, Statutes, and Commands. Our awakening and return means game over as Esau's world ends with the war of the worlds being fought and the kingdoms of this world becoming His,

"15 And the seventh angel sounded; and there were great voices in heaven, saying, The kingdoms of this world are become the kingdoms of our Lord, and of His Christ; and He shall reign for ever and ever.

16 And the four and twenty elders, which sat before God on their seats, fell upon their faces, and worshipped God,

17 Saying, We give thee thanks, O Lord God Almighty, which art, and wast, and art to come; because thou hast taken to Thee Thy great power, and hast reigned."

Revelation 11:15-17

This again is what is meant by Abba Yah so loved the world that He sent His only begotten Son to redeem it and begin the one-thousand-year reign. The Word of Yah does not return void but MUST come to pass. So Black Man,

REMEMBER who you are.

REPENT of the sins of our forefathers for not keeping the Commands of our Elohim.

RETURN to our Elohim and His Laws, Statutes, and Commands.

Only then will this nightmare end. One Love Blackman, aka Israel and Judah, aka the Whole House of Israel.

Shalom

The End

www.ingramcontent.com/pod-product-compliance
Lightning Source LLC
Chambersburg PA
CBHW070037100426
42740CB00013B/2711